# 2017
Writing from Inlandia

An Inlandia Institute Publication

# Editorial Board

**Publications Committee:**
Co-Chairs: Elio Palacios, Jr. and Glenn Williams
Lavina Blossom, Julianna Cruz,
Charlotte Davidson, Andrea Fingerson,
Timothy Green, Judy Kronenfeld

**Publications Coordinator:**
Lawrence Eby

**2016-17 Inlandia Creative Writing Workshop Leaders:**
Colton (bilingual): Jessica Carrillo
Corona: Andrea Fingerson
Ontario: Tim Hatch
Riverside: Jo Scott-Coe & James Ducat
San Bernardino: Nikia Chaney
Redlands: Mae Wagner

**Boot Camp for Writers:**
Poetry: Stephanie Barbe Hammer
Creative Nonfiction: Minda Reves

**The Tesoros de Cuentos**
Frances J. Vasquez and Rose Y. Monge
Inlandia-sponsored two six-week series of these
community enrichment writing workshops
serving an under-served community,
first in October during Hispanic Heritage Month 2016
and then again in the summer 2017.
These writing workshops were offered
at the SSGT Salvador J. Lara Casa Blanca Library
in a bilingual, bicultural format

**Executive Director**
Cati Porter

**Original Cover Design**
Julie Frenznick

**Book Layout & Design**
Lawrence Eby

ISBN: 978-0-9970932-9-2
© 2017 The Inlandia Institute and individual authors.
All rights reserved. All rights revert to author upon publication.
No part of this book may be reproduced without permission of the authors.

# Introduction

When I first became an Advisory Council member, back in very early 2009, Inlandia had just broken off from the City of Riverside and was beginning its journey to becoming the premiere literary nonprofit in Inland Southern California.

Since that time, we have more than doubled our annual program offerings, and grown our publications program from a one-book-per-year co-publishing arrangement with Heyday into a full-fledged small press, Inlandia Books. Our workshops program blossomed from one workshop into seven, not to mention Boot Camp for Writers and Indie Publishing workshops. Then, this year, we partnered with the Tesoros de Cuentos organization to offer community enrichment workshops focused on preserving the stories of an underserved community.

Inlandia has always relied on partnerships to get things done. We are, above all else, about people. Inlandia would not exist without you — attending events, participating in workshops, writing books, buying books, telling your stories, listening to the stories of others, and dedicating your time to Inlandia so that we can continue to share those stories in a multitude of ways.

As I am every year, I am grateful to all of the people who make up Inlandia. We are all Inlandia.

Every year, as we pull together to publish this anthology, I am reminded of how special this book is, and how reliant it is on the talented and dedicated writers and workshop leaders who participate in Inlandia's Creative Writing Workshops Program, a sampling of whom appear here. Thank you.

Inlandia's workshops program, including the annual publication of the Writing from Inlandia anthology, are made possible by grants from the E. Rhodes and Leona B. Carpenter Foundation, the City of Riverside, and Poets & Writers Readings/Workshops Program, with particular thanks to the director of their west coast office, Jamie FitzGerald Lahey, and the James Irvine Foundation, funder of Poets & Writers Readings/Workshops Program. We also wish to thank Inlandia's members for their generous donations of time, talent, and treasure. Special thanks to our readers for appreciating the good work found here.

We also wish to thank our host venues for allowing us to use their space to hold our workshops: the Riverside Public Library downtown, the Corona Public Library, the Rowe Branch Library in San Bernardino, the Advance to Literacy Center in Colton, Joslyn Senior Center, and the Ovitt Family Community Library in Ontario.

We are grateful for all of your support.

—Cati Porter, Executive Director

# Contents

Margit Andersson
    Homelessness — 13
Rose Baldwin
    Tropical Burger Deluxe: Chapter One of Mike's Magic Burgers — 15
Steve Brown
    True Story by a Liar — 18
Celena Diana Bumpus
    On Becoming A Pantheist — 21
    She Waits For Me — 23
    My Dearest Cousin — 24
    Tired Of San Bernardino — 26
    Signatures — 27
    Dad — 28
    San Bernardino — 30
    Silken Prison — 32
    Unbound for the Untamed Moreno Valley, Ca — 33
    Two Haikus In Homage To The Night - Pomona Art Walk — 35
Larry Burns
    For the Birds — 36
    Pinball Wizard — 37
    Monologue at Vine & Third Street — 38
Ray Carson
    A Restless Night — 40
Thatcher Carter
    Self Taught — 41
José Chavez
    '53 Studebaker in 1969 — 45
    West Coast Sounds — 47
    Roswell 1961 — 49

|  |  |
|---|---|
| The Handsome Prince | 51 |
| My Ticket to Paradise | 53 |
| A Scent of Spring | 56 |
| Road Trip | 57 |

**Sylvia Clarke**

|  |  |
|---|---|
| Sister Memories | 60 |
| Tribute Canticle | 63 |
| Katie | 64 |
| Remembering | 65 |
| The Mystery of Two Cats | 66 |
| Where Is Tippy? | 70 |

**Wil Clarke**

|  |  |
|---|---|
| Riding The Marine Tiger | 72 |
| Cleopatra of the Desert | 77 |
| Milestone in Joshua Tree | 81 |

**Deenaz Coachbuilder**

|  |  |
|---|---|
| Beloved | 84 |
| Innocence | 85 |
| love and hate on a fateful 2017 february evening | 86 |
| nature's vibrations | 88 |
| something glistened | 89 |
| The capricious ocean | 90 |
| The guardian of the garden | 93 |

**Carlos E. Cortés**

|  |  |
|---|---|
| Lifeboat Drill 1 | 96 |
| Lifeboat Drill 2 | 98 |
| The White Cliffs of Dover | 100 |

**Laurel V. Cortés**

|  |  |
|---|---|
| Inventions Vs. Families | 102 |
| The Player Piano | 104 |

**Ellen Estilai**

|  |  |
|---|---|
| Elegy for Cosmo Cool Cat | 108 |
| Within the Margin of Error | 110 |

**Nan Friedley**

|  |  |
|---|---|
| being second | 113 |

    Hand Me Downs     114
    I Read the Obituaries     115
    In the Center of the House     116
    The Last Farmer     118
    Violated     119
    You Want a Piece of Me?     121

Alexis Gonzalez
    Hope is     123
    Winter     124
    Light and Dark     125
    Once I Get There     126

Judy Conibear Kohnen
    Bugged     128
    I took the world for a walk today     129

Marvin G. Meyer
    Cooking on an Oklahoma Farm, 1920     132
    Mischief at a Country Church, 1920     135

Kimmery Moss
    Appetite     136
    Eventuality     137
    Invertebrate     139
    Nirvana     140
    Tied Together     141

Cindi Neisinger
    Evolution of the Mission Inn: Her View     142

Gary Neuharth
    Creation     145
    I Love     147
    I Remember     149
    The Boat     153

Jane O'Shields-Hayner
    The Light From Our Steps     155
    The Obsidian Mare     157

Jeanne'marie Parsons
    Am I Destined to be a Cat Lady?     158

Karl Pettway
- Intro to Reading — 163
- Winter — 165
- My First Car — 167
- Keepsakes — 168

Cindy Rinne
- Mother of All — 170

Kristine Ann Shell
- Catalina — 172
- Taking a Gamble — 174
- Mae Arrives — 176

David Stone
- Standing Ground — 177
- Rest in the Grove — 178
- Hope — 179
- Two Hollows on a Hill — 180
- At Last a Black Lily — 181

Gabrielle Symmes
- Losing Ginger — 182
- Finding Ginger — 187

Gudelia Vaden
- First Day of School — 189
- Pieces — 191
- The Season of the Empty Nest — 192

Thomas J. Vaden
- A Blessing in Disguise — 194
- Sixth Grade — 195
- The Old Shoe — 196
- Thoughts on Death — 197

Alan VanTassel
- Breakfast — 198
- Those Summer Nights — 202

Dale Vassantachart
- A Day at Joshua Tree National Park — 208

Romaine Washington
- Helium — 210

| | |
|---|---|
| When Palms Breathe | 211 |
| Ground Swell | 212 |

**Tesoros de Cuentos**
Frances J. Vasquez

| | |
|---|---|
| Tesoros de Cuentos | 216 |
| Tesoros Dorados ~ Golden Treasures | 218 |
| Parable of the Rings | 226 |

Maria Jaquez

| | |
|---|---|
| Hace Diez Años | 228 |

Morris Mendoza

| | |
|---|---|
| The Viet-Nam Era and My Block Friends | 230 |
| Memories of Madison Street | 232 |
| Relationships Through the Years | 233 |
| Tortillas and Me | 235 |

Rose Y. Monge

| | |
|---|---|
| Train Trip with my Nana | 237 |

David Rios

| | |
|---|---|
| Living in the Shadow of the Panama Canal | 241 |

Scharlett Stowers Vai

| | |
|---|---|
| Who am I? | 251 |
| What Does Casa Blanca Mean to Me? | 253 |
| Bruno | 255 |
| Alvino | 259 |

| | |
|---|---|
| Biographies | 263 |

# 2017
Writing from Inlandia

Margit Andersson

# Homelessness

To be homeless can mean several things although what first comes to mind naturally is for a person to have no roof over his or her head. It is a miserable existence, and a reminder of how much we, who have a place to live, take for granted. The political will to solve it does not seem to exist.

Another way to look at homelessness can be to see it as a mental condition. This may be even more common than the physical one although there is no way of knowing. It is a perception, the feeling of not belonging anywhere, to somehow be a misfit in society even if one's circumstances and way of life seem not so different from other peoples'. A writer, Carolyn See, expressed it once as if life is a party to which you have not been invited.

For a religious person it may seem as if life itself is not our "home", but that this will one day be alleviated and rectified. At the end of life they will finally go home, to God in heaven. My grandmother said, at the end of her life, she would soon be "home."

Sometimes home will always only be where we grew up. Where everything was right and the way it was supposed to be, life was simple, love, implied or expressed, protected us. It does not matter then if we as adults ae able to create our own family and home life. It is still not "home."

I knew of one lady who set aside a special room in her house where she placed all things from her parents' house. She said, when things went badly and life was difficult, she would go in there to regain a feeling of peace and balance.

An older woman I knew had lost all her family as well as her home where she grew up. It had been in her family for 300 years but then sold to strangers. Each Christmas Eve she walked the few miles to the old house, just to visit and see it from the outside. That deep went her attachment. She said, she spent Christmas Eve at her home.

So homelessness can be physical but also a feeling of mental estrangement, a perception that one does not really belong anywhere.

Rose Baldwin

# Tropical Burger Deluxe: Chapter One of Mike's Magic Burgers

*At Mike's Magic Burgers, the food and some of the people are magic*

Daphne Miller's feet hurt as she stood in Mike's Magic Burgers, careful to keep her slim, silk-suited body away from the well-worn wooden counter where orders were taken. She was tired of waiting by the time a fifty-something-year-old man with a short buzz cut, plaid flannel shirt, faded jeans, and soiled apron appeared. His eyes sparkled, and he had an impish, deep-dimpled smile. In spite of her peevishness, she was captivated.

"Hi, sorry to keep you waiting," he said.

Daphne felt shy and confused about what to say. After a long pause, she managed, "My assistant suggested I come here. She told me to order Mike's Special Burger, but I don't see it on the menu. Oh, I almost forgot—I'm supposed to say, 'Blanche sent me.'"

"Is this your first time here?" he asked.

Daphne nodded. "Is this Mike's? Do you have a Special Burger?"

"I'm Mike." He smiled again. "Do you like sunshine and beaches?"

"Sure," she said. Her captivation having evaporated, she added, "What does that have to do with anything?"

"I usually recommend the Tropical Burger for first-timers," he said. "The Special Burger is so delicious the bliss can be disorienting for someone unprepared." He smiled again.

This time his smile did not charm her. She was hungry. "So, you have a Special Burger that you won't sell to me because it's too delicious, and you want me to eat something not as good?"

"I'll tell you what. Since this is your first time, I'll *give* you a Tropical Burger—on the house." She made a frustrated hiss, and he added, "I'll make it a Deluxe. Find a seat. I'll bring it out."

She wanted to leave, but she had neither the time nor energy to find another restaurant. Resigning herself, she looked around. The decor (if anyone could call it that) was comprised of mismatched tables and chairs, and Naugahyde booths—some with duct-tape patches—on a floor of old checkered linoleum. The clientele was an unlikely mix of scruffy—almost dirty—people sitting next to suited professionals. An old woman sat in one corner reading palms.

Daphne chose a small booth near the front of the restaurant. Mike appeared at her side, before she'd even managed to warm the seat. Setting the plate with her burger on it in front of her, he cooed, "Enjoy," a habit she considered an annoying affectation. Cautious by nature, she lifted the sandwich with both hands and took a tiny bite. It was impossibly delicious! Taking a larger bite, she closed her eyes, and savored the remarkable flavor.

She was slightly dizzy and then felt warmth on her. Opening her eyes, she found herself on a white sand beach, looking out on a turquoise sea. The waves broke on the offshore reef, leaving only tiny surges on the beach. She saw a large man, dressed in white pants, carrying folded white towels and a basket with the pump tops of lotion bottles visible, walking toward her. Looking down, she realized that the platform she was sitting on, and had assumed was a chaise lounge, was really a massage table. She rolled onto her stomach, pulled the sheet over her, and waited.

She heard the pump of the oil and the sound of him rubbing it in his palms. Then he touched her. His hands were enormous, warm, and soft. He put one on her tailbone and the other at the base of her neck and made a small chant-like hum. Her body relaxed into a blissful calm. Slowly his powerful fingers dug into her back, tracing stiff muscles that burned then popped as they released their accumulated stress. Her mind wandered to another time and another beach as he massaged the backs of her legs, waking thighs too used to sitting for hours at a time.

She rolled onto her back.

He took her feet, which had suffered the indignity of high heels for decades, one at a time, rubbing and stretching them, working his powerful fingers into the soles. He pulled her toes and ran his finger between them, and she thought about what it had been like to be a child walking barefoot, in long cool grass.

Under his ministrations, the muscles in the front of her legs and then her arms released their stress, freeing a sweet song from her heart that brought tears to her eyes. Her keyboard-weary hands loosened; she moaned as he worked on her tired fingers, then stretched and rubbed each palm.

Finally, he probed the perpetually stiff muscles along her neck and then her face. After he finished, she lay for a long while, relishing the feel of sun on her body.

Opening her eyes, she was back in her small booth at Mike's, looking at an empty plate. Mike sat across from her. He spoke softly. "Was it okay?"

It took a moment for her to recognize him and remember where she was. She looked down at herself to make sure she was dressed (she was) and then around the room to see if people were staring (they weren't).

"Oh, yes," she said, then laughed at how deep and sensuous her voice sounded.

Mike reached across the table and touched her hand. "The Special Burger is a little stronger. You can have it next time, if you want."

"Thank you," she said.

Steve Brown

# True Story by a Liar

Once upon a time–a very loooong time ago, probably a couple of weeks ago, or maybe a century ago, or maybe even longer than that....maybe back in the days when Damsels in distress ruled the earth. Oh, wait, it wasn't Damsels, it was dragons. Anyway, there in a tall castle overlooking a beautiful green valley and a stinking polluted river that was so toxic that it would periodically catch fire,lived a beautiful young Damsel. She was such a knockout that flowers bloomed in dead grass when she walked by. If she were to kiss a pig, it would at once become a TV talk host.

One fine morning the Damsel decided to go for a walk because she was putting on a few pounds and needed the exercise. As she strolled through the woods, she failed to notice that the light was getting dimmer and dimmer. Soon she was completely lost, and crying out, "oh dear, I am completely lost." She tried to retrace her steps but since flowers had bloomed wherever she walked, nothing looked the same as her GPS battery pooped out and some graffiti idiot had scribbled up the signs so badly that they were unreadable. She was in a real mess.

She walked and walked and walked and finally came upon the strangest sight! In a gnarly hillside surrounded by blackened, twisted trees,beer cans and fast food wrappers was the entrance to a cave. Such an evil reek poured out of it that she made an ugly face. It smelled like her little brothers breath in the morning. She made a mental note to send over a bottle of Renuzit if she ever got out of this jam alive. She was so tired and cold that even this looked good, so she carefully went in. What do you know, deep in the cave, asleep on a huge pile of golden coins was a dragon.

(Start the dragon music here)

She picked up one of the coins, polished it on her tunic and held it up to the light. If you're wondering where the light would have come from, don't ask me—I don't know. Figure it out for yourself. I'm just writing this.

She looked at the coin to see if it might be worth shoplifting, but it only said one Kopek.

"Is that all?"

She griped and tossed the thing back on the pile. The clatter caused the dragon to awaken and he came to his full height. Roaring out "fe fi fo fum" he scared the bejabbers out of the princess, who asked in a shaken voice, "what are you going to do?"

"I'm going to eat you all up!!!"

By then the princess had regained her wit and yelled "you try to get smart with me buster, and I'll give you such a bang over the head you'll still be seeing stars next Christmas!" To help make her point, she picked up a blackened tree branch and brandished it *brandishingly*. The dragon, to his credit, knew when he was beaten and backed off menacingly.

What is your name?" demanded the dragon.

"My name is Aknavi lkspmurt."

"Where do you live?"

"In the castle over by the green valley."

"I thought that was lkspmurt tower."

"Correct, it is. Owned outright by Dlanod lkspmurt, the king, real estate mogul and my Father."

"Well, I'll be," said the dragon.

"You'll be what?"

"Nothing; that's just a saying around here."

"Oh, well I'll be too."

"Tell you what, you guess my name and pronounce it correctly, and I'll grant you one wish."

"I thought that was supposed to be three wishes."

"No, that's for fairy godmothers. I'm a dragon!"

After a minute's silence, she stood up tall and said, "Your name is Zoke2+0Xpurqupt<eidoidnfonoeimie>&w reimcmpel.ajotuie3394093480u;mlovkpsaefm;,x and it's pronounced the same way in Bulgarian. Easy, huh?"

"Arghrr!" screamed the dragon. "How did you do that? Nobody has guessed my name in 45,000 years. I don't believe it. How did you do it?"

"Simple. I prayed to God and he whispered your name in my ear."

With that she grabbed the dragon and gave him a big, wet kiss right on his nose. To her amazement, he turned into a handsome prince on a white horse with a Dalmatian dog at his side.

"Ok," she said, "now let's talk about my wish."

Celena Diana Bumpus

# On Becoming A Pantheist
(A Riverside Romance)

*For MSK*

While sipping a Caramel Macchiato in a Riverside cafe, I discovered Apollo sitting across the room looking inconspicuous, red-gold hair glinting in the bright lights, head tilted in contem-plation, the promise of healing in his hands.

As he glanced away from the woman he'd been watching, I realized I'd been mistaken. It was Hades instead, mourning the flight of his Peresephone, long before she'd left. He was brac-ing himself for another six months of loneliness as she returned to her other life.

In the nakedness of his pain he also reminded me of Hephaestus, a creator of such smooth, precise works of art, hiding the mystery of his scars. I wanted to offer him my hands with which to cradle his heart. My lips to soothe his wrinkled forehead. I left him a discreet of-fering, my phone number.

Eros responded to my missive instead, calling me that evening. At first he spoke of soul-mates and intensity, while I listened enthralled. He confessed he'd learned of lust from Dionysus while watching his disciples at the bacchanalia, claiming they knew the consummation of a touch, the true power behind a whispered caress. He confessed he'd had his most mind blowing orgasm fantasizing about Athena. I guess Eros had a taste of satyr within him too. Then Eros began speaking of his desire for a trusting partner, a focused mate.

One who could share his celebration of love. He'd waited patiently to give his heart, but was beginning to despair finding his "one" in his loneliness. I tried to tell him I was Psyche. I could learn to worship him. But he wasn't ready to reveal all of himself to me, speaking of promised passion instead.

In the grips of the desire he evoked, I fled his subtle seduction; hanging up to run outside and pray for perspective. Zephyrus, observing my distress, lifted me up into his arms, attempting to console me as carried me to my beloved Balboa Beach. There I found the comfort of my childhood in the taste of the sea breeze.

Poseidon swam ashore to greet me. I was happy to see him, my friend; this man who could be my father, my mentor. I asked him why I thought of candles and betrayal. He replied my destiny was not in my name and entreated me to take time to think, find myself within my doubts. He said sorrow was not my final prophecy, for I was fated to find peace. Poseidon left me sitting on the shore, staring at the ocean with the reminder of my mysterious winged god; likening the blue of the waters to the depths of the emotions I remembered within his mercurial eyes.

Celena Diana Bumpus

# She Waits For Me
(Riverside Community Hospital)

*For my mother, the better half of the collective Bumpii*

I sail past the corridors and open doors
A schooner navigating moans and cries
I dock on the pier to her room silently
Enter her room on legs used to rocking waves
She is a fragile wisp of a dissipating dream
Each inhale a gift  light as tissue paper
covering a rare, favored book
I hold silent vigil
on the metal chair next to her bed
Watching her breathe
in the pale lighthouse beams of the heart monitor

Celena Diana Bumpus

# My Dearest Cousin

*For Ivan*

    As usual it is late. I can't sleep and I have way too much to do tomorrow. I slipped away for a salty indulgence, returned with a guilty conscience. No sweets for my sweet mother.

    On the short drive through my blessedly quiet neighborhood I kept glancing at my purse--the cds I now tuck away (finally learning after losing over a hundred bootleg cds to my loving neighbors). Silence. No silence. Nothing. I have finally become decision-less.

    So many decisions and memories have crowded my waking moments. Even the brief mo-ments I've stolen for myself; after my fall, after my head injury, after my promised appearances, after my final tears, after my closing obligations, after my near collapse, after my nights of sleep-less snatches--I know that my day is never done.

    I've stopped making "to do" lists. My pages have turned into books. Rest. I don't think I remember what it is. I simply work and write until my eyes give out.

    The peace I find in Gregorian Chant music offers some moments of relief until my phone stops running the Pandora station and I am left alone and awake with my thoughts in the middle of the night yet again.

    Years ago you were my sanity--when the reality of the world broke me, broke my heart and my mind. Your love and the love of your two young sons breathed life back into my psyche.

    God! You were so shining and strong and certain and

powerful. I took one step off of that bus and I could go no further; all I could do was look up at the face that so mirrored mine and col-lapse into you. I was so weary it was a miracle I'd made it across the country.

But there you were: shining and strong, the same forehead, the same eyes, the same nose, even freckles like mine when you look really closely. If I had been born a male, I know I would have been you.

My arms did not go around you. My face didn't reach above your sternum. But I clung to you like the child I wished I could have been. The innocent that had been battered by years mend-ing shattered children.

You asked nothing of me. You didn't need to. I was kin, that was undeniable, and I was as near death as any walking and waking person could be...

Before I left for the west coast once again, we spoke of promises. I made you one I swore on my future I would keep.

Honorable man that you are, even now you ask nothing of me. But I remember my prom-ise. I remember my words to you. I remember our bond and the strength you gave me without res-ervation. Your belief in me was constant and I remembered my vow.

I give you everything I have left. I give to you--my belief, my faith, my magic, my es-sence, my prayers.

I will be what I vow to be for you. I will give you what I promise unconditionally. Because I love you and we are family.

Celena Diana Bumpus

# Tired Of San Bernardino

Classmates I kept tripping over
The Ponderosa on Echo
Living alone in the guest house
Living alone in the fourplex
    Across the street from the elementary school
    Where a teacher's husband dragged her out of her class at gun point
    And shot her point blank
Two buildings down from the working girls
    I spoke with everyday on my way to university
Living alone in the duplex
    Across from the small house where my mother lived
    Nights my toad would bark like a Chihuahua
    All of my freshwater tanks gurgling to cover the
    Silent cries of the angelfish and tiger barbs as the sharks nibbled at them

                                            In between meals
    My California Rosy Boa nestled in the terrarium across from my bed
        Not eating rat-cicles because the live food would beat him up
    Chirping crickets gobbled by my Fire Bellied Toad
        Who never cares to share
            Cheerfully murdering any reptile that shared his terrarium

Celena Diana Bumpus

# Signatures

Lately, I've left parts of myself everywhere. My pink fetish dripping from my neck, arms and legs. Reminders of the years I fought for my life in the Chao Family Cancer Center at the University of California, Irvine Medical Center at Orange, Ca. Who are you to tell me I don't see the world in mauve-colored glasses?

I hated pink as a child. Refusing to be defined by that one weak color. I thought I was so much more than that. Tell me what smart, self-assured woman wears pink?

It's just been in he past two years that I realized how strong pink can be. I never realized there were so many beautiful hues of pink. I began religiously collecting the six hundred scarves I amassed after I host my hair to chemotherapy.

Strangely I never wore a scarf during my three months in Egypt after my treatment. My husband would not allow it. You are not a true believer he would tell me.

So many signature colors I had through the years. Red was my favorite color as a child. I would bounce around in my favorite red patent leather sneakers; matching them with any and everything, sometimes wearing clashing colors.

After graduating from high school, I discovered the enigma of black, and how it nurtured the unfathomable side of my Gemini psyche; later, I integrated grey and army green. My attempts at being inconspicuous still left me standing out in a crowd.

I never liked neon pink. It was too pretentious a color for me to take seriously. It reminded me of watermelon. Of slavery.

Celena Diana Bumpus

# Dad

*For Jerry Wayne*

 I ran into your obituary the other day as I was packing to move to my new place. I had tucked it into a box of treasured things that hurt me to look at. I told Mom what I'd found over breakfast the next day.
 You were the well-read and life taught. Sharing and exploring the lives of others over beer. You were the youngest child of a patriarchal family; proud of your confident baby girl.
 You were birthday cards when I was a child. The phone calls I made when I was confused about men. You were the keeper of memories and the family researcher— finding our ancestors coat of arms. You were the only one to call me "princess" and God how you loved to brag about my grades in school, the gifted programs I excelled in, the instruments I could play. The awards I won the jobs I scored. I even became the youngest director of Goodwill Southern California, in San Bernardino and Palm Desert.
 And then you were the man with two other children you neither claimed or loved. The hard-drinking, temperamental, taciturn man with resentful opinions about everything and everyone. The ice bitter "I-should-have-done-more-with-my-life" loner still dependent on your older siblings for approval. The manipulative "you-don't-love-me-enough" swallow of guilt I choked upon every time you ask me to live with you longer. You were so possessive I suffocated in your arms and yet you never felt you were good enough—felt pressured upon to show you were smart enough— to have a daughter like me. You were the black sheep that taught me I could go

against the grain and still be true to who I am. You were the one that showed me how I needed to control my life so I wouldn't fall into an abyss of depression. You were the one that who showed me long-term relationships are possible with interracial marriages. You were the one who swallowed your guilt after not speaking to me for years with your final words to me the night before you died, "Forgive me. I've always loved you. I was always proud of you." That night I finally learned to call you "Dad".

Celena Diana Bumpus

# San Bernardino

What a wasteland of lost potential
the dry earth like burnt toast
except for the long slide of native grapefruit slices
slithering down my parched throat
picked fresh just steps from our front door
at the Ponderosa on Echo Drive
        Fertile land tilled, raked, watered and nurtured
        by my Grandfather Bill's kelly green thumb
        He could coax the largest pomegranate
        from the most luscious bush

All of my plants drowned screaming accusations
in sludge in the scorching desert sun
forgotten projects of a fruitless planting lesson
        If I could cast a spell to bring Seattle's rains
        to this land with its dry dusty soil

        The land fight so hard to stay barren
        I cried to my grandpa

                He said, Darling you'll get the hang of growing plants
                You just haven't found the right plant yet

As usual, grandpa was right
office plants became my specialty

But there are no blooming grapefruit trees in cubicles
The skeletons of Grandpa's orchard still languish abandoned on Echo Drive

We grandchildren make pilgrimages regularly to pay homage to those lost lush days

Celena Diana Bumpus

# Silken Prison

Morning opened with the Tallis Scholars
wild birds were harmonizing with Gregorian Chants
I awoke slowly  listening
my impromptu avian choir chattered discordantly
I put on Jesse Cook
salsa and merenguing across the bedroom
opened my curtains  the first time all year

My avian music critics departed
cracking the window slightly
the air like sheets out of the washer tasted crisp
*fresco* like raw celery

Inside scents of fresh ginger  chicken  lime
Earl Grey undertones
programming the Marley boys
Ziggy  Stephen  Damien
I gyrate and pirouette back to the windows

My silken scarves frame
window's view
vibrant greens  ripe vermillion fruit
oxidized mercury sky

Day on the verge of exploding
the ignition  the Santa Ana winds

Celena Diana Bumpus

# Unbound for the Untamed Moreno Valley, Ca

*For MM*

I arrive at the witching hour
hold him under the night sky
until his tears slow
their cascade down
the right side of my head
through my hair
onto my face

He alternates between
taking deep shuddering breaths
and inhaling the scent of my hair

I love the way he imprints
my scent into his memory
every time he sees me
I always surprise him
with a new scent to him
of me besides the familiar

Freeing myself
from his tightening embrace
I put a hand on his heart
look up up up at him

It was his nose that first
drew me to him
Large, straight and long

as his jet black hair
Which is bound in a low ponytail

Holding me tight to his side
he leads me into his lair

Celena Diana Bumpus

# Two Haikus In Homage To The Night - Pomona Art Walk

Fresh crisp night, warm smiles
skip effortlessly nimble
delightful embrace


Black shrouded party
goers hop over shimmering
iridescent pools

Larry Burns

# For the Birds

On Sunday morning the birds
Que in neat
Aggregate rows. Sparrows
Flit around the rooftop
Poking out the mud nests
They took from the
Swallows. Mourning doves,
Always in even numbers,
Watch patiently from
Powerline perches. Blackbirds
Too, but most hide just out
Of view, appearing
In huge flocks when
Instinct and experience rings
The dinner bell.

Larry Burns

# Pinball Wizard

I retreat
From the world in fearful acknowledgement
That I cannot control the world
And struggle to find even a reason
To control my self.

The pinball machine is a marvelous machine.
An apparition of lights, levers and sound.
Large box with a glass top, a world
Complete.
And self-sufficient. And I am its god.

Here is control. The outcome
Not always predestined
The ball eventually drains
But I know why it does when it does.

Larry Burns

# Monologue at Vine & Third Street

"At the place they'd tell you to go over there for biscuits and gravy.
Biscuits and gravy, that's what they eat.
And when they come out they say,
'Oh no, I'm gonna be sick!'"

[he bends over like a butler]

"That's what they say when they come out; that's what they do.
I saw, come out and say,
'Oh no, I'm gonna be sick!'
I learned that about 5 years ago, you know."

[he wanders off, out of earshot, talking back and forth]

[he turns back]

"I see the coins.
Pick them up, out in front of the church,
they're lying on the ground.
I put them there, all over the place, just lay them out.
Come out of church and put them there.
I've never been inside, can't because I'm not invited in.
Because I look at the ground a lot.
Dale has a metal detector, finds all kinds of coins, hands full of coins.
Maybe I should do that too.
Because I look at the ground a lot. So this guy is chasing me with a flashlight.

And I tell him there's a nail in the tire, there's a nail in the tire.
Then I keep going because he might have something else in his hand.
Know what they would do to me in Ontario if I had that in my hand?
Not in Ontario.
Knife or a gun in my hand, that would be. Then his pants are coming down.
Expensive pants you know what can happen to those.
So I kicked his pants off so I could know where he was, keep him down there.
But if I had a knife, or a gun in my hand, a gun.
I would probably use it."

[he points his finger and pulls the trigger]

"I wouldn't get one but if they gave me one I'd use it.
Shoot at the…the ones going by.
And yes, I'd point it, or a knife."

[he stabs]

"Yes?"

Ray Carson

# A Restless Night

    I went camping by a lake one week-end with a school chum when I was about 14 years old. We thought it would be fun to take some cigars to smoke, neither of us having had much experience with tobacco so it sounded fun.
    Once we were all settled in our camp site, my Dad was gone and it was dark, I broke out the cigars. I lit one up and inhaled a big draft of smoke from it. We didn't know that people don't normally inhale cigar smoke, but simply chew on the end and puff a bit. At any rate, the large volume of smoke in my lungs triggered a severe fit of coughing like I never experienced before or since. My lungs hurt all night. I think that was my last cigar ever.

Thatcher Carter

# Self Taught

I can't remember my parents teaching me how drive, but I do remember getting in a car accident the first day I got my license. Related? I'm not sure, but when my son turned sixteen, I'll tell you, I wanted to be the best driving teacher the world had ever known.

I watched you tube videos and reviewed DMV pamphlets. When I was ready, I drove him to the Sears Roebuck in Riverside, CA and stopped the car in an empty corner of the expansive lot. I told Max to get in the driver's seat, and we did a thorough check of rear view mirrors, hand signals, windshield wipers. Then, I had him release the parking brake. Our minivan glided down the gentle slope of asphalt without him even touching the gas. I hadn't planned it, but Max was amazed. "I didn't know that would happen," he said. Score one for the parent knowing more than the teenager, except I hadn't known that, and don't you dare tell him.

We spent weeks driving and parking and turning and signaling. I set up soda bottles on our suburban street and had Max back up until he thought he was as close as he could be without hitting them, and then we'd rush to the back of the car to see how well he'd done. We didn't have rear cameras or driver's assist, and my lessons were designed to help him understand blind spots and mirror perspective and precision. When we got on the open road and he accelerated too much or braked too suddenly or too close to the car in front of us, I thrust out my leg to its imaginary brake and grabbed the armrest. I may have gasped a few times, but I would always remember what my friend, also the mother of a teen boy, told me, "They may not make the best decisions, but they have amazing reflexes." I can't explain how much this calmed me. I imagined Max's survival instinct overriding his distracted mind, his synapses firing straight to his muscles, bypassing his teenager brain, and getting his foot to the brake just in time.

The freeway in California requires a herculean set of nerves for a parent riding with their child. For my son, I let the state-required driving instructor take my son careening on the 91 West on his first lesson, and I happily stayed home. However, for my daughter, four years later, I was in charge of the task because Emily was seventeen-and-a-half, and the state did not require teenagers of that age to have any formal instruction. None. And she didn't want my instruction anyway. "No way," she said. "Max warned me. You're the worst."

The worst? How was that possible? To me, I had been calm, Zen-like, prepared. Through their toddler years, I had been flying by the seat of my pants, reactionary and frustrated, I would admit that, but the worst at driving instruction? I couldn't even hear it.

I finally convinced my seventeen-and-a-half-year-old Emily to let me take her driving. She needed practice with a licensed driver even if the DMV didn't call that instruction. I was able to take her to Sears Roebuck and intentionally let the car glide when she released the parking brake. She wasn't nearly as impressed as my son had been, but I still ran through the paces of how to signal and turn, how to inch out in the road to see cross traffic clearly, and how to make a U-turn.

Near my husband's birthday, we decided to go to dinner in a town twenty minutes away *on the freeway*. My daughter, still not eighteen, held out her hand for the keys. I didn't want to be the worst, so I got in the passenger seat while my husband got in the backseat, eyes glued to his phone for the entire ride. I gave Emily as much instruction as I could in the few blocks from house to freeway, but when she sped up the on-ramp and tried to merge into the next lane, she looked over her shoulder and let our car drift out of its lane. We were going sixty miles per hour, and my half of the car was in the wrong lane.

I could have told her, "Slow down" and get in the lane behind the SUV next to us. I could have told her, "Speed up" and get in front of the car the next lane over. I could have yelled "Stop" because the car in front of us had slammed on its brakes. But all of those would have scared her, alarmed her, taken out of her own intense concentration. What I probably needed to tell her was to trust her instincts, it would all work out, even a failure wouldn't be fatal. In actuality, I couldn't croak out anything other than, "Okay, okay, eyes forward. Stay in the lane." Sweat sparkled on my forehead, and I felt real fear, almost a panic at how far we had to go on this eight-lane freeway. I kept inching over to the middle of the car to avoid the feeling that we were going to hit the cars speeding along on my side. It was hard to be a passenger after being a driver for so long.

When my son got home from his second year in college, my husband was recovering from a terrible car accident: drunk driver, no warning, broken collarbone, months of recovery. He used his insurance money to buy Max a $4,000 pick-up truck. Only problem, it was stick shift, and Max didn't know how to drive it. My teacher antenna went up, and I raced out to the truck to be his instructor, once again. It was a loose clutch, which required lots of practice to perfect the timing between gas and gear. Max stalled a few times on our street and one time in the middle of an intersection. I waved to the other drivers and talked Max through the process. "A little more clutch. Step on the gas. Okay, third gear."

A few days later, after several instructional trips with me and his dad, Max came in from the driveway and said triumphantly to me, "I basically taught myself how to drive stick shift." I thought he was joking, but he went on. "I watched a few videos, and then boom, I had it." I didn't say anything at the time or any time since, but I was bemused he had written my instruction out of his mind. He had become self-taught.

And of course, I look at my own driving record, and what's the one part I can't remember? My parents ever teaching me to drive. I remember borrowing a car and burning out the clutch because I didn't release the parking brake. I remember speeding tickets and the day I decided I couldn't afford them anymore. I remember my own car accident and having to fill out the insurance paperwork. My parents must have helped me. It was their insurance after all. And now, right now, as I mull over my disjointed driving experiences, I remember a moment I had as a new driver. I was sitting at a red light waiting to turn left into a parking lot or a strip mall in the suburbs of Illinois. As soon as the light turned green, I stepped on the gas and started to turn. My mom put her hand out; I can't remember what she said, but she stopped me. Cars were coming up the road, and I was about to turn directly in front of them. I thought I had the right of way. It would have been a certain accident, and my mom, in the passenger seat, would have taken the brunt of it.

She must have had a sparkle of sweat on her forehead, and maybe she blessed my teenage reflexes that I was able to stop in time. Maybe it was a story she shared with her friends. But her instruction had faded to the back of my memory, and my driving had become a story of my own trials and errors, my own triumphs and revelations. That's how I introduced myself to you, as the woman who couldn't remember her parents teaching her to drive.

Teenagers are a mass of instinct and reflex and *sui generis*. They are teaching themselves themselves. Every time they step on the gas pedal or slam on the brakes. Every time they write us out of their memories and continue down the road. Every time they get turned around on the streets where they grew up because they're used to seeing them from the backseat and now they need to relearn the landscape from the driver's seat. We're learning, too, because nothing looks the same after you've taught your teenager to drive.

José Chavez

## '53 Studebaker in 1969

A lustrous chrome grill grins and waits as I
adjust the mirror on this blue hard body.

The Commander model, strong, tough, proud,
like they used to make 'em in Detroit.

Eight-track tape player with only one speaker
inside the dash, a groovy selection of electric

tunes next to me. One hundred thousand
miles strong, steady without power steering.

Don't need cruise control as I glide bien suave
from east LA on a Sunday afternoon. Let that V-8

swing, rattle, and roll me west on Santa Monica Blvd.,
toward the pier. Windows down, everybody digs

my ride, blasting Santana and Hendrix, except
for two chicks navigating the Pacific Coast Highway,

pretending not to notice brown curls and ocean breeze
blowing my natural hair piled high and round.

Sailing a beige Dodge Dart, they're dreaming about
surfer dudes in loud Chargers, Mustangs, and Firebirds.

Maybe a '53 Studebaker isn't cool for two blonds,
I guess it's not every girl's dream car.

Makes me no difference,
Don't cut no ice with me,
lotta horses under my hood,
Carlos and Jimi ridin' shotgun.

Look in the mirror—yeah,
I got this.

José Chavez

# West Coast Sounds

A melody rides on the high tide
you can feel it where the sun sets in Venice.
A familiar tune follows you
on a quick stroll before you meet friends.
Feel the purple glow deep
in the western horizon.

Savor a moment, the crash of each wave
as it rides closer, ever closer to your bare feet.
Sound echoes in your ears as you remember
                the steady beat of *Good, Good Vibrations*.


Blue-winged seagulls and brown pelicans
zoom low above your head, and beat their
wings in harmony with each step. Just past
the jetty you'll join your *amigos* and share
fruity Sangria and a warm April fire.
                remember *All Day Music by War.*

We'll talk about the old days at Santa Monica College
Martín graduated and works in Long Beach,
Christian survived the surfing accident
at Redondo, Martha and David—
always together, did they ever get married?
                the Doobies sang *Listen to the Music*

Inhale ocean mist for your lungs,
smooth rhythms for your toes,

and embrace the pulse of your soul,
With each step, chase the wet sand,
and yellow moon rising in the eastern sky.
> *How Deep Is Your Love?*

remember,
remember,
Like a dolphin, surf the next pounding wave,
> the sound will carry you in.

José Chavez

# Roswell 1961

Dusty streets on the staked plains,
crooked cottonwood tree up front,
rough gravel in the driveway.
I can almost see Texas from here.

Walked to Grandma's house last night
with little sister, plenty to eat there.
Warm flour tortillas, stuffed
with spicy green chile and papas.

Friday morning at Pecos Elementary,
and I wonder if Mrs. Johnson
will be nice today. There's a
long stick for those who don't obey.

Kids in bunches before the bell rings,
playing marbles or soccer,
watching 'em score goals
through a metal frame without a net.

Lunch time and I already know
about refried frijoles
between two slices of white bread.
Hide this from sharp eyes.

Milk is only ten cents,
but water sounds good today.
I like the taste of water,
"*No hagas un escándalo,*" says Mamá.

Back to the two-bedroom
home for nine of us.
adobe walls break through
plaster missing on the side.

My turn to bring water
for an afternoon bath,
A red metal hand-pump out back,
gotta find the metal bucket.

Fifteen minute boil on the stove,
don't mind bathing in the kitchen,
Mamá helps me pour the water in the tina.
Glad no sisters are watching me bathe.

Outside to play with our cocker-spaniel mix.
I tell him I want to ride horses
and be a cowboy like Roy Rogers.
He grins at me and I think he believes me.

Spanky likes chasing cars, and I
don't know how to make him stop.
A good scolding awaits when he does it,
but one night, we carry him off the street.

Now I sit on the curb and wait
for Dad to come home. When he's late,
I look for smooth pebbles to roll
into the street, and keep waiting.

Where's is he? Not coming home,
I guess. Mamá says it's payday,
a long afternoon for all of us—
and still a longer weekend.

José Chavez

# The Handsome Prince

*They were married that day
and lived happily ever after.*

Let me explain some things:
she was a beauty alright,
but not used to being
away from her family.

Nights in the spacious castle
were restless for her,
as dreams quickly turned
into nightmares about
seven strange dwarves
moving in with us,

playing with half-sisters
who hated her,
fleeing an evil queen,
and spinning straw into gold
under sentence of death.

It took its toll.
I'm paying for joint therapy
sessions, and we both watch
Dr. Phil every chance we get.

Just had my checkup,
and was told to stay away
from rich foods and watch
cholesterol levels.

Our fourth daughter
is getting married soon,
imagine the royal
bill for that wedding.

My therapist says,
**Happily ever after**
is a relative term.
I tried to ask her

what the hell that meant.
She quickly smiled
and handed me the bill.

Lesson learned:
handsome and charming
only go so far.

José Chavez

# My Ticket to Paradise

This summer I wanted to find something more than a "vacation", something to last, a unique experience, something with a "big wow" factor. Asking a friend over the phone for ideas, or simply checking websites online, wouldn't work for what I had in mind. I called my travel agent, explained what I was looking for, and made an appointment for 2:00 pm.

I told Shannon I was looking for "Paradise", so she showed me locations with the usual palm trees, umbrellas in the sand, attendants bringing fruity drinks with little orange umbrellas—not what I had in mind at all! I've nothing against two carefree weeks on a tropical island, but I've been to Los Cabos, Costa Rica, Jamaica, and similar places. Now I'm wondering if I'm really asking way too much. Maybe she'll suggest a simple writer's retreat, or virtual reality glasses.

She didn't. Knowing that I write poetry, I was surprised to hear her describe a new tour geared to writers and poets. To boost their economy, Puerto Rico was offering a new Paradise Tour, exclusively for writers from all genres and styles. We had a lively discussion, and after viewing amazing photos, I quickly paid for the trip, and gave her a hug before I left.

Two months later, I downloaded my ticket, and flew on Trans Caribbean Airlines to Puerto Rico. My hotel accommodations at the Tropicana were first class, as expected. After breakfast, I took a short walk past majestic palms and cobblestone streets, and there it was.

At the mall called: *La Inspiración*, everything was dedicated to books and writing. Just outside the entrance to the two-storied structure, I was greeted by a spirited trio playing smooth island rhythms, and songs by Jose Feliciano. A group of local street artists were finishing a mural dedicated to the memory of the indigenous Taino people. Local farmers were selling mangoes, yuca, whole coconut with a straw, and slices of fresh pineapple. In front of the entrance, there was a stand with a banner that read, "*Bienvenidos Escritores*, Welcome Writers." A local writer, and one from Cancún, were there to greet visitors, and ask a few questions about my writing genres and experience.

Stepping inside, I noticed only book stores, libraries, and newsstands. Some stores sold new books in the traditional fashion, but most were independent stores owned by writers who came to visit, and never left. There were Five Dollar Book Stores, One Dollar Book Stores, and Leave a Book/ Take a Book stores. Intrigued and impressed, I wanted to continue exploring.

It was exciting to visit kiosks where poets gave directions to your favorite stores, after reading the poem of the day. They mentioned that there were readings five times a day at the food court. The theme this week was poetry by Pablo Neruda. Next week the readings would feature writings from Victor Villaseñor, with Maya Angelou the following week.

The food court, itself, was even more amazing as you could find tacos and arepas at the Latino Writers Bistro, fresh sea bass from the Ernest Hemingway Grill, and soul food at the Langston Hughes Harlem Buffet. There was an open mic every night of the week at the Café Robusto and Tea Garden. Walls were covered in murals by Diego Rivera, paintings by Frida Kahlo, Monet, and Picasso. There was a large dining area dotted with tables, chairs, and comfortable couches. In the center atrium, there were were statues by Michelangelo, Bernini, and local artisans.

Words could not describe what paradise felt like at that moment. How does a poet uncover a feeling, or color an emotion? I can't remember a Christmas Holiday or my birthday ever being this exciting. I knew I had to call my wife to make arrangements for her to get here fast! As for my children, two of them are already writers. The third loves computer games, but I know there's hope.

I recall what Shannon had said the day I bought the tickets. There are no refunds for this tour, she explained, but neither are there are blackout dates, no inflated holiday rates, no passports, a speedy security line at the airport, everyone flies first class, and once approved, you never have to leave.

How do you get approved for Paradise? That story is for another day.

José Chavez

# A Scent of Spring

At Bull Run, Union troops scurry across hills
in panic fleeing the southern charge.

At Chancellorsville they fall amid
a crack of heavy musket fire.

At Chickamauga men in grey are cut
to shreds by grapeshot and canister.

At Fredericksburg twelve-pounder canons
gouge holes in the hills above town.

At Gettysburg men in blue coats shiver
at the sound of the rebel yell.

Charge after furious charge, the standard bearers
fall. Souls are bent, broken, and shattered.

Neither curses nor prayers console bodies
on a slope called, **The Little Round Top.**

Blue and gray uniforms mix, blend, fuse as one
in a terrible forever embrace.

An April haze on the summit greets wild daisies,
while the scent of spring fills their bones.

José Chavez

# Road Trip

Road trip,
road map
road sign,
road crossing,
road destruction,
road construction,
road hazard.

Road inspection,
road protection,
road entrance,
road exit,
road west,
road inland,
road taxes.

Roadies,
roadie rowdies,
rowdy roadies,
road tires,
road warranty,
road weary,
road rage.

Road confusion,
road somewhere,
road anywhere,
road everywhere,
road nowhere,

road closure,
lost road.

Old road,
new road,
toll road,
free road,
road you're on,
road you seek,
road you wait for.

Road to Hollywood,
road to hopes and dreams,
road to the stars,
road to freedom,
road to happiness,
road to easy street,
road to Heartbreak Hotel.

Road of life,
road of love,
high road,
road of peace,
road of comfort
road of forever,
road to Shangri-La.

The slippery road,
flooded road,
coastal road,
desert road,
mountain road,
forgotten road,
long and winding road.

Road not taken,

road taken,
fork in the road,
gravel road,
dusty road,
mangled road,
broken road.

The road home.

Sylvia Clarke

# Sister Memories

I have a new baby sister! Her name is Elvina. I'm going to see her today.

Daddy said, "We're going to Butte." That's where she's at the hospital with Mama, and we can bring her home for Christmas. I'm so excited I can't wait!

But Butte is a long ways away, and in the car I get wiggly and make Daddy go off the road into the ditch. There's snow in the ditch. Daddy gets out to find a way back onto the road. I sit crying and thinking, "My fault, my fault!" A tear-stained face looks back at me from the shiny dashboard buttons of our old black Chevy.

After a while Daddy comes back, stomping snow off his boots. He says, "I think we can get out just up there," and points to where a farm road crosses the ditch. He starts the engine. I shut my eyes.

Once we are on the road again, I open them and stare out the side window and try to imagine my baby sister. I see her as a little brown haired doll. A red ribbon holds back her long hair as she dances around the Christmas tree. Do I know what a baby really looks like? Sure, but I can't help thinking of baby Elvina as a doll I can play with.

A few weeks later when I try to pick her up off the big bed where Mama has laid her, I learn otherwise—especially when Elvina wiggles, and I drop her on the floor. Uh-oh! I didn't mean to hurt her. She cries, and Mama and Daddy run in to rescue her—and deal with me! I remember.

My 9th grade year, Elvina and I were enrolled in a private school 35 miles from home. Mom worked as a nurse in Flint, and Dad was a pastor, so neither of them could drive us to school every day. One of Dad's parishioners, Marie Day, came to the rescue. Her son Rollie also went to Tri-City Junior Academy, so every day Marie picked up Fern, a 10th grader, Patty in 6th, Elvina, 5th, and me in her big green Packard.

What a mix of teasing and chatter she put up with as she faithfully drove the five of us the 70 miles to and from school. This arrangement meant that Elvina and I not only shared a bedroom, we were together nearly all the time except for school hours. Conversation often included bits like this:

"Mornin' Spitball!" Rollie slid over on the front seat to let me in beside him.

"Hi, Rollie. Uh, Marie, will we get there early today? I need to talk to Mr. Barger before class."

"What you need to talk to him about?" Elvina piped up.

"None of your bees wax!" I flung at the back seat where she was getting settled.

Fern's quiet voice joined in. "Oh, she's probably gonna make sure she got yesterday's history assignment. She doesn't always pay attention in class." Fern and I were both in Mr. Barger's 9th and 10th grade classroom.

Patty giggled.

By this time we'd be on the road and soon on a bigger highway. "Hey!" Elvina shouted. "There goes a red convertible. Wanna guess how many we'll see before we get to school?"

"Ten!" Rollie liked high stakes.

"I'd guess maybe three?" I'm usually conservative if I guess at all. This was a game we all played at times, but Elvina enjoyed it most and was the best at spotting those red convertibles. So the time usually passed pleasantly on our long daily rides.

As a 5th grader Elvina seemed to feel quite grown up and managed to have two different boyfriends during that year:

Joe and Mike. I actually saw her walking on the playground holding hands with at least one of them. I wondered at the time what Mom and Dad would think. But I never told them. She did that herself. She shared, "I kissed Mike," saw Dad cry, and learned *you don't tell them everything.* Poor Sister.

When Wil and I moved the family to California 30 years ago, we were not only near Wil's dad and step mom and his brother Elwood, but my sister Elvina also lived within visiting distance. For many years we had seldom been together, and in some ways I felt she was a stranger. We had missed so much of each other's lives. She married a psychiatrist and had two boys. I married a university math professor and had three children: two girls and a boy.

Of course we love each other, and as we spend time together, our adult friendship grows stronger. One day as we shared childhood memories, Elvina said something I will never forget: "Oh, so you are one of *us*, not one of *them!*" Unfortunately, during our growing up years, I had been what some called a goody two shoes, and our parents had at times held me up as an example. Now we were discovering that each of us had suffered under this type of parenting—and regretted it.

Elvina's unexpected statement brought a bond to our relationship that has strengthened over the years. No, we don't think the same on everything or always agree, but we can relax with each other and enjoy life's moments, many of which are worth remembering long afterward. Isn't that what sisters are for?

Sylvia Clarke

# Tribute Canticle

Almighty God, our just King,
    Blessed be Your holy Name.
Creator of everything,
    Descending to earth, You came

Expecting nothing from me--
    Forsaking glory above,
Giving your own life to see
    How we respond to your love

Infinite, given, and free
    Just to bring all life anew.
Kindness and grace You decree
    Leavening all that we do.

Merciful Father of all,
    Never forsaking Your child,
Open our ears to Your call.
    Put us where we, undefiled,

Quietly rest in Your grace
    Ready to do Your command,
Seeking to look on Your face
    'Til in Your presence we stand.

Undo our pettiness, pride;
    Vanquish all self-seeking sin.
Work in us as You abide
    X-raying all that's within.

You are our Helper, our Guide,
    Zealous to stay by our side.

Sylvia Clarke

# Katie

She sits, alert, ears half pricked,
    sleek side rubbing my leg,
        lis'ning to sounds in the neighborhood.

A jet's overhead rumble
    attracts her eyes skyward.
        If she sees it or not, I can't tell.

Evening zephyrs sway the trees;
    a palm branch creaks nearby.
        She stands up, puzzled, head swiveling.

A car passes in the street;
    "Woof-ruf-ruf!" She gallops
        to the gate to watch it disappear.

Lizard sunning on the wall,
    canine scents in the grass ...
        For Katie, life is fascinating!

Sylvia Clarke

# Remembering

    My life-long best friend:
Like a prince he strode ahead
    curly auburn hair
setting off deep-set blue eyes
that twinkled and smiled at me.

    His confident stance,
belying shyness inside,
    led me at a glance—
intrigued--to query, study,
and later become his bride.

    More than fifty years
we've faced all kinds of weather,
    shared each other's fears
and joys, the pain not counting,
just so we walk together.

**I love you, Wil!**

Sylvia Clarke

# The Mystery of Two Cats

Two tiger-striped grey kittens, brothers it turns out, came to live with an expatriate couple in a country far away. Sharon welcomed their company since her husband Henry's work often took him away, leaving her alone at home. She found her cats a comfort at those times. As the kittens grew, their mistress noted how they enjoyed each other, sitting together on a mat, chasing one another around the house, and sometimes sleeping next to each other on top of the large covered hamper in the hall.

When they were together, it was easy to tell these cats apart, for one was larger than the other. Besides, the smaller one had a peculiar circular stripe on its left shoulder. As they grew, their owners provided, along with food and a litter box, an opening through the screen on a small window where they could come and go as they pleased in the wider world. This was only done, however, once they were full grown and more able to take care of themselves. Before that, Sharon usually locked them in the house while she was gone to protect them from the untamed dogs that often ran loose in the neighborhood. How they yowled and complained then, becoming very insistent about wanting to get out, Sharon's neighbors reported.

One day, they both disappeared and failed to come home after their night out. In fact, they were gone several days. Sharon worried about them and searched the whole area, calling them by the sounds she had used to tell them dinner was in the bowl. No response.

How she missed their company. She wondered what had happened to them. Then one early morning, the bigger cat showed up, exhausted, hungry, and extremely nervous. He jumped at any noise or quick movement. Sharon could only guess what had frightened him. She did notice a worn place around one leg, as if it had been tied with a string—a common practice in the country where she lived. Had both cats been stolen? If so, how had this one escaped?

After a day or two of rest, the cat that had come home became restless. He meowed loudly at his mistress, asking to go out—not the way provided but through the front door. When she let him out the door, he ran quickly toward a nearby wooded area, stopped, and looked back as if asking, "Are you coming with me?" Sharon followed him to the edge of the woods but then turned back. It was already evening, and she didn't know how far the cat wanted to go. Besides, she wasn't dressed for a long walk—or one in the wetness that followed an afternoon rain. The cat emitted a long, loud, frustrated "Ye-o-owl!" when Sharon turned, walked to the house, and went inside.

For weeks, this remaining cat, Big Cat, would disappear for a day or two—sometimes even more, and the restlessness increased whenever he was at home. Each time he returned exhausted, with burrs and seeds in his fur and an ever more watchful attitude. Did he know where his brother was and go to visit him? Or was he just looking for the lost brother? Mystery and more mystery.

Finally Sharon decided she really must try to follow her cat and see what she could learn. Big Cat seemed overjoyed. Bounding ahead meowing, he then looked back to make sure she was still coming. When sure she was following, he'd run again, flopping down to rest at intervals while he waited for her to catch up. They came out of the woods onto a dirt track, crossed fields and a paved road, headed into a forest, and then followed along a railroad track.

Meanwhile, Sharon called Henry to join her, and the two of them continued following Big Cat after dark—that is, until the batteries in the flashlight gave out. What a howl of disappointment greeted their ears when the cat discovered they were giving up the trek. It was as if he pleaded, "You can't give up now! We are so close!"

On this trek, Sharon figured they had walked between four and five kilometers. No wonder the poor cat came home exhausted and hungry. So many dangers threatened him: people walking by, cars on the highway, ponds and streams to avoid. The mystery deepened, and Sharon knew she must try to follow him at least once more and find out what had happened to his brother.

One late afternoon Big Cat's excitement grew when he realized Sharon planned to follow him again. Waving his tail back and forth, he began gleefully meowing as Sharon set out behind him, going past the garden and into the woods. They followed the same route as before, and a little later Henry and Joel, a young man who knew the local language, joined them. Eventually all four came to a group of tombs above the nearby village.

There Big Cat nosed around each tomb, sniffing at the grass and the stones, meowing loudly as if calling his brother. Then he sat down on top of one of the tombs and waited and waited. "Astrologers use cats in some of their ceremonies," Joel explained. "And they usually perform them at night near the ancestors' tombs. Maybe your cat is waiting to see if his brother will come here."

After some time, Big Cat jumped off the tomb and headed toward another rise where more tombs stood. He followed the same sniffing, meowing, and waiting routine he had used at the first set of tombs. By this time it was well after dark and getting late. Sharon, Henry, and Joel decided it was time to abandon the search and return home. Picking up Big Cat, they headed to where Henry had parked the car near the village.

The cat's reaction surprised them. When they picked him up, he became totally limp as a rag doll. He did not struggle but allowed them to enter their vehicle with him in their arms and lay motionless during the ride home. As the car door opened at home, however, Big Cat sprang to life, jumped out, and disappeared into the dark. Sharon never saw him again. Soon she began to notice some differences in her life.

For the previous year or more, Sharon had been suffering from ailments that no doctor could diagnose or treat. She had even traveled to her home country to consult doctors there, but nothing helped. Courageously, she had carried on her work and supported Henry in his responsibilities. Now, however, after both cats disappeared, she felt much better and even declared, "There's a totally different atmosphere in our home!"

Slowly Sharon began to put together small incidents that had occurred when the cats were living with her. She remembered that whenever she and Henry knelt to pray, the two cats disappeared to another part of the house. Once when she was sick in bed, the cats kept her company—that is, until a group of friends and colleagues came to pray for her healing. As they entered the room, the two cats immediately jumped off the bed and exited.

The kittens had been a gift. There had been no suspicion of problems at first. Now Sharon began asking why. Why had the person given her those two kittens? Had they been cursed by some local diviner or astrologer and given to provide a portal for evil forces to enter her home? Did she need to be wary of all gifts presented for no apparent reason? These and other questions arose. No certain answers could be found. In the meantime, however, Sharon and Henry are grateful for a more peaceful home and lessons learned from "The Mystery of Two Cats".

Sylvia Clarke

# Where Is Tippy?

"Mama, where's Tippy?" Panic edged my ten-year-old voice as I dashed through the back door into the kitchen where Mother stood at the sink washing apples. Our curly-haired black dog almost always met me when I got off the bus. Today he hadn't. Then, I remembered the still black form at the edge of the road I had glimpsed from the bus window. "I think Tippy's dead!" I wailed.

Mother dried her hands, took me in her arms, and asked gently, "What makes you think that, Dear?" I haltingly explained what I had seen. "How far away was that? Mother wiped tears from my cheeks.

"I think it's just past the old barn at the end of the garden," I sniffled.

"I'll go with you to find out what happened," Mother soothed, patting my shoulder. Leaving sister Elvina to stay with Judson, our baby brother, Mother and I started out the door and up the driveway to the paved country road that passed our little green shingled house. Just as we stepped onto the edge, a loaded logging truck rumbled past, shaking the ground.

"You don't think he got run over, do you, Mama?" I remembered all the times I had walked along this very stretch of road with Tippy happily running ahead. He always ducked in and out of the blackberry vines that grew along it, sniffing, exploring, tail wagging like a flag.

"We'll have to wait and see," Mother replied as she took my hand in hers. Past the garden, the brambles, and the collapsed barn we walked until something black and furry ahead caught our attention.

I hung back. Did I really want to see what happened to Tippy? My stomach turned, and I lowered my eyes while Mother used her foot to turn our beloved pet enough to expose the broken flesh, the blood, and the mangled insides. One peek and I knew for sure I would never walk or run with Tippy again. Mother's eyes became misty, and I broke into sobs.

As we slowly walked home hand in hand, I finally whispered, "Couldn't Jesus have kept Tippy from getting run over?" The question hung in the air.

Wil Clarke

# Riding The Marine Tiger

The year was 1946. Fred and Esther Clarke were only two of the thousands of Americans who had been missionaries scattered throughout the world. They had served in South Africa since the beginning of 1936. German U-boat activity during World War II had made returning home impossible. During the war most of the United States merchant ships had been converted to warships in the eventually successful efforts to win the war. At the end of the war the United States government stepped in to help bring Americans home.

The Marine Tiger had originally been designed as a passenger ship but was converted into a troop carrier by the time she was launched in 1945. (In those days ships were referred to by feminine pronouns.) In 1946 she was sent to South Africa to fetch as many Americans as desired to return home. She docked in Cape Town first and then sailed east around the southern tip of Africa to Durban where she completed filling up with passengers. The Marine Tiger's crew was composed of marines filling out their tour of duty before returning to civilian life. At each stop the ship made, a number of the sailors would go ashore, get drunk, and never make it back on board before the ship sailed.

As the ship pulled out of the Cape Town Harbor, everybody stood on deck in a very festive mood. Friends on shore held one end of long paper streamers while the passengers on board held the other end. The idea was to see whose streamer would last the longest. When a streamer broke, people would hastily tie the fragments onto the ends of one that was still intact. At last all of the streamers broke as the Marine Tiger headed out to sea.

Fred and Esther had been in Africa for over 10 years. They experienced the pain of separating from very good friends. But there was also the excitement of being able to reunite with family whom they hadn't seen in those 10 long years away from home.

Passenger families were separated for the long voyage home. Women with small children were housed in the officers' quarters, and men were housed below where the troops would have travelled. The children of one family had colds, sore eyes, and runny noses. Within short order all of the children on board had colds, sore eyes, and runny noses, including me. Because of my 18 months old brother Elwood and me (Wil), Mother Esther stayed in the officers' quarters with us. I was just over 4 years old at that time.

Each deck had two rails around the edge to keep people from falling off the ship. Early in the voyage, little Elwood stood right against the rail. He placed his heel over the steel lip of the deck and then pulled his foot back. He watched pensively as his shoe fell fifty feet into the harbor. Of course he had only the one pair of shoes; after all, the family had been living on a scant missionary salary for more than 10 years. Fortunately another family on board had a child who needed only the opposite shoe, so they split the pair between the two kids.

Elwood had no fear of heights at the time. One day, after the ship had been out to sea for several days, an officer came into the cabin and said to Esther, "Is this your child?"

"Yes!" Esther sounded shocked. "Where did you find him?"

"I went out on deck and here was this boy. He had crawled through the railing and had his feet on the deck and was holding onto the rail with only one hand and leaning out over the ocean, staring down at the foam running past below. This scared me half to death. I crept up silently and reached over the rail and grabbed him with both hands." The officer was as white as a ghost and trembling from the experience.

"Thank you!" Esther was now pale with fright. She went to work and fashioned a harness for Elwood. It restrained him for the rest of the voyage.

Dad used to love to walk out to the bow of the Marine Tiger. He would lean over the steel prow and stare down as she sliced her way through the water. On occasion he took Elwood and me out on the foredeck. There he stood Elwood up on the prow, and Elwood loved it. Of course he held onto the child very tightly. I was old enough to have a healthy fear of heights. To this day I still remember the terror I felt as Dad held me up on the prow and let me watch the plume of water fifty feet below.

The ship's crew went all out to celebrate the Crossing of the Line (the equator, of course). Several days before the crossing they busily stretched a rope net down the starboard side and under the ship and back up the port side. Anyone who hadn't crossed the line on some previous voyage was informed that they would have to climb down the starboard side, go under the ship and climb back up the net on the port side of the ship. This scared me. I knew that both Dad and Mom had crossed the line before, but of course I hadn't. Dad tried to reassure me, but that did little to alleviate my dread.

On the great day of the Crossing of the Line ceremony, passengers and crew gathered on deck. One giant crewman was dressed as the god Neptune. Another was dressed up as the goddess Salacia, Neptune's wife. He had a giant bogus bosom stuffed into a makeshift bra. Several of the experienced crew stood about, tridents in hand, to shepherd the novices one by one onto the deck. The novice had to crawl up to Salacia on his hands and knees. She would ask him his name. When he opened his mouth to answer, a crewman would stuff a large paintbrush with a quinine solution into his mouth, choking him with the bitter concoction. Then he was forced to crawl through two bent air vents that were fastened end to end. At each end of the vent stood a sailor with a powerful stream of sea water gushing through a two inch fire hose, forcing the victim through from one end and impeding his progress from the other. I remember the crew gave us cookies and candy afterward and a certificate that we had been duly initiated.

On her way to New York City, the Marine Tiger stopped at Port of Spain on the island of Trinidad for refueling. The sailors hadn't been ashore for over two weeks, and they dashed off the ship in glee to enjoy the usual sailors' amusements. By the time she was ready to sail, fewer than half the sailors had made their way back on board.

A powerful tug, the pride of Port of Spain, attached a very long rope, thicker than a man's arm, to the bow of the Marine Tiger. It towed her out at least two miles into the Caribbean. Standing on the top deck with my parents to watch the departure, I could hear the captain on the bridge swearing louder and louder. He kept expecting the tug would disconnect from his ship. Finally he ordered full speed aft. The great engines of the Marine Tiger roared into action. The ship shuddered under the mighty strain. As the ship and tug pulled in opposite directions, the rope between them pulled up out of the ocean. Water poured off it as when one rings a soaked towel.

Dad yelled, "Watch out! The rope's going to break?!" It did. I watched as part of the rope shot back onto the foredeck. Anything that was loose on the deck was flung out to sea. Fortunately no one had been stupid enough to stand down there; it certainly would have cut them in half.

The Marine Tiger arrived in New York with about a third of the crew still aboard. It was not a happy homecoming for our family. Two telegrams awaited us. One was from Mom's sister-in-law stating that if she did not come out to Phoenix immediately, she would not see her brother alive. The other was from Dad's sister saying that if he did not come to Michigan immediately, he would not see his mother alive. Esther's mother had died just six weeks before they arrived in America.

We caught the train to Michigan immediately but arrived only in time to find his mother lying in state. Although I was only 4 years old, I still remember seeing my grandmother lying in bed. I believed that she was just sleeping. It took a number years and a lot of arguing by the older people to convince me that she must have indeed been dead when I saw her.

Right after my grandmother's funeral, Mom took Elwood and me with her on the train to see my Uncle Bob who was extremely ill with asthma. We stayed with him for a number of months to help my Aunt, who had to work every night as a waitress. Years later Mom used to say that their homecoming was an extremely sad occasion. I think it had to be a real trial of their faith.

Wil Clarke

# Cleopatra of the Desert

Cleo was old. Her hips were failing her solid body and sharp mind. She had lived with us and the desert across the street for all of her life. I was deeply saddened to watch her steady inexorable decline. She had a harder and harder time getting into a standing position from lying down. We put rugs over the slippery floors to aid her, but we knew this would only be a temporary measure.

We dubbed her Cleopatra when she was about six weeks old and we took her away from her black German shepherd mother. This blood made her ready to fight at the first sign of competition. Her father probably had a lot of black Labrador in him, but he had absconded to Mexico after he got her pregnant without leaving any contact information. From her father Cleo got her loving and accepting nature towards all our friends and their children.

When we first brought her home, Cleo was roughly the same size as our four-year-old Lucy, who became a very dominating mother figure. Both of them could run in and out of the cat door in the bathroom. Lucy would gaily steal food from right under Cleo's nose. I watched with curiosity to see how long Lucy's air of superiority would last.

About a year after we got her, Cleo towered over Lucy. One day I had the good luck of being in the kitchen when Lucy dove in boldly, as always, and snatched a morsel from right under Cleo's nose. Cleo looked nonplussed for a few seconds, realized her size advantage (60 lb. to 12 lb. Lucy), and then with a deep throated roar, took off after Lucy. Surprised and scared half to death, Lucy dashed around the kitchen—dining room—living room circle, yelping her terror. Cleo dashed around after her rumbling her threat of vengeance. I practically rolled on the floor laughing at this development. It took several minutes before Cleo gave up the chase. Needless to say, Lucy never again tried stealing another morsel from under Cleo's nose.

Cleo would never readily tolerate a door that kept her from going where she wanted to go. She watched us open a door using the door handle. She found that she could often open a door by standing on her hind legs and placing both front paws over the handle and pulling down on it. I watched her do it many times to get either out of or into the kitchen. When that didn't work, she would bite the door handle and try to twist it with her mouth. When that failed, she would try more desperate measures: digging up the carpet in our bedroom, ripping the door apart in Julia's room and the bathroom, and tearing the molding off of the garage door. She also learned to open the front gate by jumping up and pushing the latch open. She never tried to run away, and if she inadvertently got left out, she would lie down at the front door and whimper until we let her in again.

Almost every day we would put leashes on our two dogs and then walk the 300 yards to beginning of the desert hills. There we would unleash them, and they dashed around excitedly while accompanying us up one or another of the trails into the La Sierra Hills in front of our house. During the all too brief winter rains, the foxtail and cheat grass would grow rapidly, produce seed, and then die. The annoying grass seeds would get in Cleo's feet and ears. They would stick in Lucy's fur as well as feet and ears. Fortunately the annoying grass seed season wouldn't last more than a month at the longest.

No matter how long the drought, the desert always seems to produce rabbits and coyotes. Cleo had a nose for rabbits. On occasion, while I was toiling up the La Sierra Hills, she would suddenly dash under a bush. It never surprised her when she would come back out of the bush with a rabbit in her mouth, brains crushed by a single bite. She usually devoured it skin, fur, bones, and feet on the spot. This would take less time than it takes for me to write about it.

Cleo regarded coyotes as mortal enemies. She probably out-weighed them by twenty pounds and would chase them eagerly at every opportunity. She never caught one, actually seldom got very close to one.

The desert hills have a super abundance of giant boulders, many of them tilted at threatening angles. It seemed that the slightest push would send them rolling wildly down the hillside and into the frail homes in the valley. However, it is very evident that they have retained their precarious positions in spite of all the earthquakes that have frequently shaken the Southland. For me it was always a challenge to try and scale the boulder we were near. The cliff faces of the boulders were often quite smooth almost everywhere, presenting a challenge to climb them and enjoy the elevated views in every direction. When I achieved the top, Cleo would whine and walk around the boulder a few times, looking for an easy spot to climb. If she found none, she would take a run and scramble up the vertical slope where I had climbed it. Amazingly, she usually made it to the top. Lucy would simply sit below and yap.

Deserts also sport sharp objects like thorns on almost every tree and shrub. Snakes, especially rattlesnakes, and scorpions have stinging and sometimes deadly sharp points. As we were walking along a desert valley trail near our house one day, Cleo suddenly stiffened and gave a high-pitched bark. She reserved that particular bark for one thing only: a snake. She started to lunge towards a wild desert buckwheat plant that was covered in white blossoms accented in pink. I called sharply, and Cleo obeyed immediately but reluctantly. I grabbed her by her collar and pulled her back from the bush. Under its dark green branches a large western red diamond-back rattler lay in wait. It raised its head, and its beady little eyes looked straight at us. Its rattle beat a well recognized warning. I put the rubber tip of the walking stick I was carrying right up into its face. It struck, but only half heartedly. As I continued to poke, it refused to strike again. All it did was slowly retract under the shade of the bush.

As she approached her fourteenth birthday, Cleo developed arthritis in her hips, a common occurrence in many large dogs in this country. We fought it for almost two years with a daily pill of glucosamine/chondroitin that she would take and chew up before swallowing. Our vet had suggested using this human dietary supplement for a previous big dog of ours. The pill seems to prolong their ability to walk and run for at least 18 months. When Cleo was almost 16 years old (that's about 110 doggy years), she finally gave in to the ravages of time. She died the end of March, and we still miss our "Cleopatra of the Desert" very, very much.

Wil Clarke

# Milestone in Joshua Tree

August 2016 I contracted West Nile Virus. After nine weeks of hospital and rehabilitation stay, I was barely able to walk, unstable on my feet, and suffering from constant headaches. I regard steps in regaining my former abilities as milestones in my recovery. Since then I have re-learned to walk and can even take fairly short hikes into the La Sierra Hills near our home. God has been more than good to me in the process.

On Monday June 12, 2017, my wife Sylvia and I accompanied my brother Elwood, my niece Sonya and her family, and a friend, Dalel, to Joshua Tree National Park. Prior to my bout with West Nile Virus one of my favorite pastimes was scrambling on rocks and boulders. My extremely weakened muscles and my balance control troubles have precluded any rock scrambling since my illness, so I hiked—slowly—whenever we went there. This time I had decided to attempt to climb something easy yet significant. I set my sights on scaling a hill back of Barker Dam that is mainly comprised of a massive granite rock that is fairly smooth yet challenging.

Barker Dam Trail threads its way between granite outcroppings that we call kopjes. We attacked the first kopje on the left of the trail. It is really a huge pile of granite boulders that I used to climb easily in my pre-West Nile days. Currently I have neither the strength nor control to be able to scale a vertical face. After dragging myself up several minor boulders, I reached a point where I could go no farther. I just didn't have the necessary physical strength or balance.

Coming back down from the limited height I had obtained, I dropped onto the top of a large boulder below me. Bad move. My weak legs didn't allow full body control. Fortunately the boulder was large enough for me to run a few paces and regain my balance. Had it been a bit smaller I probably would not be writing this because I would have fallen off its edge. I proceeded down onto the desert floor with much greater caution.

The rest of our party continued to scale that kopje while Sylvia and I walked along the trail towards the Dam. As I rounded a bend and came out from under a live oak tree, I looked up to my left. High above us on a gigantic boulder next to the trail posed two desert big horn sheep, perfectly still. Their features stood out in exquisite detail against the clear blue sky. Over the last thirty years that we have visited Joshua Tree once or twice a month, we have seen desert big horn sheep only eight or ten times. The first thought that went through my mind was that they must be a sculpture erected by the national park, but I knew that was ridiculous. Then a third sheep came into view, and the others turned to look at her.

My heart leapt within me. They were real. What a great start to a day of achievement! I called to my wife, Sylvia: "Look at the big horned sheep."

"Wow! What a treat!" She scrambled up a rock to get a better look.

Going a few paces farther along the trail, we got a much better view of them. There were two ewes and one half-grown lamb. As we watched, another lamb the same size stepped into view on the rock. Then a great ram came up behind the lamb. His magnificent horns spiraled a full 270 degrees. He exuded pride and satisfaction as he surveyed the family he had shepherded onto the boulder. They all regarded us with bored curiosity. People are a common sight to the sheep around Barker Dam, but the sheep rarely allow people to see them. In awe we sat and feasted our eyes on the sight for at least half-an-hour.

After a brief lunch back at the cars, our party of nine headed back along the trail. One of the ewes was still visible on the boulder; the rest had gone their own ways. Two weeks previously I had walked up the steep, wide granite hill I had chosen as my goal for today. I had reached a point about 40 vertical feet above the desert floor. On that day the extremely hot sun and lack of breeze caused me to turn back. I knew I didn't have the energy to go the distance. It was a good thing that I did because by the time I reached the car that day, I was totally exhausted. I would never have made it back from the top of that kopje.

On this Monday the weather was cool, and a delightful southwesterly breeze whisked our sweat away. I started up the broad flaky rock with Elwood on my left, Dalel on my right, and Sylvia spotting me at the back and encouraging me. I didn't need them, but they did give me a sense of security. About two-thirds of the way up, Elwood and Dalel left to guide the rest of the party through the maze of rocks and passages that ran the length of the summit. Sylvia and I took another way and reached the high point. This was the second thrill of the day. I finally arrived at the goal I had set for myself. I was back on the rocks and had survived. So far.

A normal Clarke aspiration is to not only climb a great rock but also come down by a different route than we had used to climb up. On the opposite side, the great granite kopje is fragmented into cliffs, and hundreds of boulders lay piled at random. The descent probably took us an hour and was considerably more challenging than our ascent; but it was aided by the fact that at least gravity was now on our side.

What made it even more beautiful was the presence of a score of different kinds of blossoming plants from the tall prickly pear to the humble mat flower on the desert floor. All of these were blooming in spite of the lack of any appreciable rain since February. The sighting of flowers and the unexpected view of big horn sheep simply added joy to my celebration. I had achieved another milestone in my journey to full recovery.

Deenaz Coachbuilder

# beloved

she waited for him to return
pretending to be busy
not acknowledging
the hours

when she heard the key turn
her heart, singing in the air,
flew to greet him, her very breath
calling out his name

his feet across the silk Kashmiri carpet
created a sonata
of whispering stars, throbbing
gently within her ears

he called out to her
his words imprisoning
her heart
with mystical cords

he turned the corner, her eyes
drowned in his presence
like a bee lost among
a lake of lotus flowers

Deenaz Coachbuilder

# Innocence

Elegant olive green plumeria leaves
curling into their burnished brown undersides
lay scattered beneath the tree in our front yard.
He selected one, a gift for me,
and placed it on a prominent spot in my room.

Olive soon turned pale and the brown began to crumble.

Once a leaf separates
              and falls,
it fades away
        and becomes earth.
New leaves and blossoms will take their place in the spring,
    I assured him.

He is four, and cannot accept the inevitability of death.
With tender care,
        he places it
under
   the "mommy" tree.

Deenaz Coachbuilder

# love and hate on a fateful 2017 february evening

two Indian men
in their thirties
both engineers
met after work for a beer
at a strip mall
in Austins Bar and Grill
where they were well known

a man walked in
accosted the two friends
"get out of my country"
the T V was loud
they ignored him

but
he was back with a gun

shots rang out

one immigrant, Srinivasn,
a Hindu
was on the floor
dead
the other wounded

Brad removed his shirt
and tied it tight around Alok's
leg to staunch the bleeding
Ian was shot

trying to intervene

a few days later, Srinivasan's wife
Sunaya said they
had so many dreams…
they love America and wanted to
do much for "this" country
her heart broken

now he is every where
  and no where
his clothes
his side of the sink
she thinks of the way
he used to brush, shower
he was a very loved child
his father's
trusted son
she said
  as her voice
faded
  into
    a whisper.

On Feb. 22nd. 2017, in Olathe, Kansas, two legal Indian immigrants were shot by a Caucasian man who hurled racial insults at them. Srinivas Kuchibhotla died, while Alok Madasani and Ian, a bar patron, were hospitalized.

Published in ladylibertylit.com/single-post/on2017-08-18/his-fathers-trusted-son

Deenaz Coachbuilder

## nature's vibrations

*There is an unexplained connection between
all living things…Deenaz*

she stopped
and stretched out

her hand
to a wild thing

it broke its stride

with soft words
she spoke

with silent gaze their
incandescent souls
built a bridge

with the speed of
darkness
the forest stilled

nature's starry raiment
enveloped them
in its
binding cloak

Published in *The Avocet*, Spring 2017

Deenaz Coachbuilder

## something glistened

something glistened
in the early light

she looked
just as majestic as before

her crown
made jagged
in the struggle for freedom

her torch
the world's beacon

the eternal flame
of blinding beauty
bestowing enlightenment
to all

her flowing gown
a welcoming river
to the downtrodden

'tis nothing,
just the tears
on lady liberty's face.

On January 28th. 2017, President Trump's executive order closed America's borders to refugees and immigrants from seven Muslim-majority countries.

Deenaz Coachbuilder

## The capricious ocean

The ocean chooses to be what it wants to be
while eternity ebbs and flows.

Anticipate the tides as being predictable in
    time
        mass
            force
 but are they?

Ebb tide… early in the morning, the ocean recedes
back into its benighted kingdom
laying bare the bruised sand
to helpless dying sea creatures… the broken shells
of brittle star fish and sea cucumber.

Days after, it decides not to show up until later
choosing to fool families
laden with mats and picnic baskets,
keeping in abeyance their well laid holiday plans.

It drowns out the sky with malevolent intent
covering the expectant sand with darkly tinted cobalt waves
disguising silver shells waiting to be plucked.
But in the evening, sunsets of golden magenta,
cerulean and rose madder bleed into its currents
churning all into heaven's painted melting pot.

Sometimes, with a heart of gold, the ocean
gently nudges the bare toes of worshipping children,

kissing their cheeks with drops of ice cream foam.
Like a magnet, it draws down the sun that leaves the waters
shimmering with a thousand tiaras
and children's faces etched in glittering reflections.

On the darkest of nights when street lamps cast a lonely light,
it is there with its winding streams and gliding tributaries,
hidden and quiet, barely submerged beneath the surface,
lurking snakelike to lunge
                        suddenly
onto the unsuspecting shore.

Sailboats skim the sinuous surface.
Majestic cruise ships prepare to leave port for fabled destinations.
Fishermen cast their nets while blessing the abundant ocean.
Precious cargo is transported across a thousand miles
enriching sender and receiver. Undulating waves
rub shoulders and laugh with delight as the sky
touches the shore. Lovers murmur sweet nothings
in a heady embrace along the twilit sand.

I gaze with watchful eyes, knowing the capricious nature
of those heedless waves, whose subdued force
can carelessly crumble rocks into sand.

    Did not
        your tsunami
            killer waves
                destroy
                    the peaceful
              coastal
              communities
        from Indonesia
    all the way
        to Thailand
           over to

Sri Lanka
    and into
India?

Deenaz Coachbuilder

# The guardian of the garden

When you walk into her garden, you do not see the sculpture.
Turn right, there it stands with the San Bernardino range as its backdrop,
positioned beside pink sand stone steps, surrounded by clusters of roses.
The tip of a giant California coast redwood root carved into the head of a venerable man. A touch of gold wood shades the face,
tangled whiskers and flowing beard, deep set eyes.
He seems to wear a crown the color of ash.

At dawn, she looks out the bedroom widow to witness Aurora's eyes
transform his wet darkness with the first rays.
She walks towards him on quiet evenings.
With respect, she touches his rough bark.
She does not need to speak.

They lived along the California coast, an impressive stand lining
the Pacific Ocean. From the Sequoia's highest reach, peregrine falcons keep watch.
The sweetness of sunlight burnishing the tree's huge crown of multi green needles,
filters among hundreds of branches.
With raised arms, it touches heaven's starry panoply.

They say, hidden in the canopy, is a complete forest ecosystem of soil and water,
plant communities, mammal habitats, birds and amphibians.
Imagine the sounds of birds-woodpeckers, jays, warblers and

owls,
wing to fluttering wing; fledglings learning to fly, then returning,
sheltered in the heart of this great being. Tree squirrels gracefully leap
from branch to branch. The red tree voles nibble delicately on fresh green needles
while the redwood's roots sink deep into the soil, shunning the harshness of sunlight,
supporting legions of worms that aerate the earth.

Lovers sit under the shade. If they quarrel, the tree shakes ominously.
When they kiss, leaves and soft pine needles shower them in a healing whisper.

The seasons brought rotations of death, and renewal,
    and then,
        a final goodbye.

They say it's been two thousand years.
    To the redwood it seemed    but two, when it heard
the early whispers of farewell. The spotted owl was the first to hoot a warning.
Long time resident warrior and black ants reluctantly began their long march
down rounded swellings of burls, irregular red brown ridged bark, following
its long tapered trunk to the wet carpet below. Then fled those beloved birds
leaving behind their hard wrought nests in haste, followed by panicking squirrels.

The marrow hidden in the tree's spine began to shake and tilt.
Blistering gales, floods and rains had washed away its

strength.
Roots anchored deep within the earth unfamiliar with the light, upturned,
fragments scattered. Evergreen forked branches laden with pollen cones
cracked and crushed beneath its weight.
                    It dropped
                              to the forest floor.


Though the clean line of redwoods is broken,
    the tree is not dead.
Living again, it carries time's secrets transformed into sheltering walls,
sturdy beams, patio tables and chairs, burls carved into multitudes
of lasting beauty, even the woodchips a boon to humankind,
    a sculptured bust.

For a while the redwood sculpture languishes in a shed amidst
numerous carvings hidden in the back row, tucked into a corner,
the days of sunshine and birdsong almost forgotten.

A door opens. A ray of sunlight touches it, swirling around like a halo.
The figure of a woman blocks out the glare.

The spirit of the California Redwood rushes forward…
    mesmerized, she is drawn towards it
  the root absorbed into her heart.

He is the guardian of her garden.

  *-Dedicated to Joan Koerper, passionate preserver of nature.*

Carlos E. Cortés

# Lifeboat Drill 1

Cruise ship lifeboat
  Tiny
  Tinny
  Taunting

Hunk of suspicious metal looming over us
Mandatory lifeboat drill resounding
Cruise ship captain intoning
Loudspeaker failing

"In case of a real emergency . . ."

Lifeboat ominously rusting
Bow more fragile becoming
Oblong windows contorting
Seats shrinking
Corrosion spreading
Vessel dissolving

"There will be plenty of seats, food, and water."

Faces ashen turning
Limbs shaking
Butts expanding
Disbelief spreading

The boat now grinning
   at our confusion
   at our apprehension
   at our consternation

The grin widens

Carlos E. Cortés

# Lifeboat Drill 2

Welcome to the lifeboat drill.
Please listen carefully
As this may save your life
When the ship goes down.
Excuse me, *if* the ship goes down.

During the lifeboat drill,
You must refrain from
   Talking
   Smoking
   Drinking
   Farting
In case of a real emergency
Such behavior, especially farting,
may cause you to be denied boarding.

I will now read the list of passengers for lifeboat station 12.
Answer as I call your name
Unless you can't understand what I am saying,
In which case, please look for another option.

In a real emergency,
You must bring your life jacket to the station.
Your jacket is probably somewhere in your stateroom.
In the meantime,
If you need further instructions for putting it on,
Your room steward *may* be happy to help.

You must be orderly when entering the lifeboat.
If you need to push others overboard
So that you can find a seat,
Please shove them over the port side,
As passengers enter from the starboard side.

Does anyone have any questions?
Actually, I don't know anything more,
So if you want additional information,
Please contact your travel agent.

Have a wonderful cruise.
It is too late for a refund.

Carlos E. Cortés

# The White Cliffs of Dover

Our May, 2012, three-week round-trip cruise from Rotterdam to Portugal, Spain, Italy, and Gibraltar started well. On the first afternoon Laurel and I serendipitously teamed up with a couple from Bethesda, a woman from Vero Beach, and a former Florida sheriff to form the Spermologists, a trivia juggernaut that would dominate the daily team competition. This included usually besting our main rivals, The Rotweilers, who had reigned supreme on the positioning cruise that had brought the ship from the United States to Rotterdam.

To savor our initial victory I relaxed alone with a glass of Chardonnay on the starboard side of the top deck, gazing southwest at the impenetrable mists toward what-should-have-been England as the ship rocked and rolled through the English Channel. Then, suddenly, unexpectedly, the mists evaporated, the clouds rose, and the White Cliffs of Dover exploded into view, seemingly near enough to touch.

The bloody White Cliffs of Dover! I can't enumerate the number of times we had cruised through the Channel without ever glimpsing those cliffs, sometimes because of weather, other times because of darkness. But there they stood: erect, sparkling, daunting, beckoning.

The challenges of living -- indeed, the problems of the world -- disappeared as I relished the ship's relentless sway and stared at the vertical face of the chalk cliffs, even more brazenly dramatic than I had ever imagined. I don't think I turned away once -- or even blinked -- for the next hour, as I basked in those mesmerizing moments of complete escape and total peace.

Then came the dreaded announcement.

"This is your captain. You are all to proceed at once to your lifeboat stations for the mandatory emergency drill."

Our station was on the ship's port side, facing southeast toward France. By the time the drill ended and I hurried back to the starboard deck, the cliffs had disappeared. I had experienced my first and maybe my last glimpse of the White Cliffs of Dover.

Laurel V. Cortés

# Inventions Vs. Families

There was laughter 'round the campfire;
then someone invented the wheel.
We were gathered 'round the hearthside;
electricity ruined that deal.

We lived in well-lighted homesteads;
Model T's whisked the husbands away.
We planned a nice family picnic;
Junior split in his hotrod that day.

We *all* cracked up at radio's comics;
TV made its sneaky debut.
Now it's reruns of Downton Abbey for us
While *they're* glued to ESPN II.

Sure, we all used to eat at the table;
home cooking's not fast enough now
"I'll pick up some fries and a pizza!" (cringe);
he'll fill up his stomach somehow.

Our kids used to charge around the kitchen;
now "chargers" keep up with the fads.
Every outlet's attached to some strange device
be it cellphones or laptops or PADS.

Do not hire one more technical genius!
Don't invent one more earthshaking thing!
I don't want one more space-gobbling gadget!
(Nor one pill that turns winter to spring!)

They've destroyed all the fun we experienced
when we sat by the campfire's glow
together in laughter and gossip,
accepting life's true ebb and flow.

Great inventions *will* disrupt the family;
they've been doing it right from the start.
It takes wisdom to maintain a balance
so that change doesn't tear us apart.

Laurel V. Cortés

# The Player Piano

The old oak upright player piano sits against our living room wall, loaded down with various musical instruments: an army bugle, a clarinet, maracas, a wood block from Nicaragua, an Andean flute and a ukulele. My beautiful Gemeinhardt flute fell (or was pushed) behind the piano years ago, my granddaughters recently confessed.

The piano is too loud for the room, too heavy to move, and too full of family history to have towed away.

At the turn of the 20th century, the piano was a bride's gift for my mother's Tante Sula (Aunt Ursula), purchased by her husband to give her companionship when he moved the city girl from Omaha to his cattle ranch in the remote high desert of Wyoming, ninety miles north of Cheyenne. After dinner, when she played the Western songs the cowboys taught her or pedaled piano rolls ordered from the Sears Roebuck catalog, the piano became the ranch's most important source of entertainment.

In 1918, Tante Sula asked her sister Josephine (my grandmother): "Jo, why don't you bring the older children with you to homestead a parcel of land adjacent to our property. Then after five years, when you have proved up the 160 acres, we'll buy it from you. You'll have the money, and we'll have a larger ranch."

My grandmother said "Yes!," which would not come as a shock to anyone who knew the adventurous Schmidt women. Their sister, a "spinster" (Tante Lena to my mother), traveled the West alone as an itinerant secretary--to Denver, Boise, Kansas City, Chicago, or to wherever temporary secretarial service was needed. She was a great source of envy for my grandmother.

Their mother, Maria Michelsen, had come alone to this country from Itzehoe, Germany (near Hamburg) as an indentured servant to a family in Omaha. When the 25-year-old woman disembarked in New York everyone was crying. She thought to herself, "Even in Itzehoe, as bad as it is, everyone isn't crying." She spotted a newspaper featuring the picture of an ugly man framed with a black border. Although she knew no English she bought the paper, which is still in the family archives. Maria entered the country the day after Abraham Lincoln was shot. He had died at the dawn of that day, on April 15, 1865.

And so it was that in 1918, when my mother was 12 years old, my grandmother Josephine tore her out of her middle class life and her beloved school in Omaha (she was a classmate of Henry Fonda) to live in a flimsy homestead shack in the middle of nowhere. The property had no running water, no protection from heat or cold, no electricity. Worst of all for the scholarly girl, there was no school! Natalie was devastated. As the eldest child of seven, much was expected of her, and to her my grandmother showed neither kindness nor compassion.

In time, although she still lived in and had duties in the shack, Mom was put to work on Tante Sula's ranch, which was a blessing. Her solace was the piano, because at least she could continue her lessons under the tutelage of her aunt.

Among the cowboys that my mother fed and worked with was a family of young boys. They were mourning the recent death of their eldest brother, Russell who--at the age of only 19--had returned from The Great War with mustard gas poisoning. He went off from the homestead to die alone, knowing the horror that awaited him and wanting to shield his family from such memories as he himself endured. Russell's loss was agonizing for his 10 siblings because he was their hero.

But the homestead boys were resilient, and their mischievous cowboy humor revived. My mother *needed* to laugh, and she became great friends with them all. Her grounded intelligence and natural optimism retuned when she was with them Natalie gladly played for the Vermilyea boys on that player piano in Wyoming. Eleven years later she married one of them, my father, Veblen (after Veblen County) Platte (after the Platte River) Vermilyea. My mom was 12 and he was 10 when they became friends. She asked him how long he had been working--sunup to sundown. He said he didn't know, he'd been working all his life.

All my father asked of his wife when they got married in 1929 was that she give him a Christmas—throughout his 21 years, Christmas and other holidays had been just workdays like any other. Our mother saw to it that he and their eight children and 15 grandchildren enjoyed fabulous Christmas seasons for the next 64 years of his life. He was a jovial Santa in a Stetson hat and through the years always had an eager group of little elves to help him distribute the many gifts.

\* \* \* \* \* \*

My parents brought our family to Carlsbad, California in 1942, and Tante Sula, now widowed, soon followed. Naturally she brought her player piano with her. Upon her aunt's death, my mom brought the piano into our crowded house. Later she entrusted it to me—along with 42 piano rolls--when I got a home of my own.

    In the mid-fifties in Carlsbad when I was in high school, the band kids used to come over to our house for taffy pulls and to sing to the piano rolls. My sister Gloria, our friend Gladys Ferris and I pedaled and sang in harmony this silly song   (Who could forget these last two verses?):

> "T'was a perfect day that brought my way
> A perfect bundle of charms
> And I had to grin when dimple-chin
> First went to sleep in my arms

Let the sunshine keep on scorchin'  
Let the heavens pour down rain  
In my heart I own a fortune  
On Happy-Go-Lucky Lane."

Ellen Estilai

# Elegy for Cosmo Cool Cat

You sauntered in sideways, your crooked tail an unheeded warning that our life would be askew, awry, a cosmic chaos of screen doors shredded and sofa arms rent relentlessly, an extended catastasis in search of a climax, a concatenation of catastrophes.

Tuxedo cat, more Frank Sinatra than Cary Grant, more insouciant than innocent, more boho than tuxedo, your reputation preceded you—the snatching of sandwiches from the hands that fed you, the baiting of thugs in the parking lots of LA (not for you a city of angels), the scars and oozing sores. Just temporary, we thought, this exile to the suburbs away from your nemeses. "Of course, we'll take him," we said. "We'll save him from himself."

Nothing could contain you. You were a black and white blur in every doorway.

Our vet, who came to know you well, would smile and murmur, "Oh Cosmo, Cosmo, Cosmo," and stitch you up again. He tagged your chart: "Difficult Cat." Nail trimming technicians encircled you—two, three at a time they came--- but were vanquished. "We tried. We really tried."

Our Thanksgiving Day entertainment, you tripped out on tryptophan, catatonic. Not sure what to wish for, we held a mirror to your muzzle. "No, still alive," we said on many more than nine Thanksgivings, far more than we bargained for, far more than the odds.

Vaulting across our sternums at midnight, clawing our heads at 4 a.m., pacing behind our pillows, you would not be ignored, single-minded, restless, reckless, insatiable. Food when you wanted it, sliding door in and out and out and in and in and out when you wanted it. There was little to recommend you.

Little, except your heart, earnest and true, and that dog-like way you skipped along beside us, and the three or four hours after lights-out when you gave up your quest and nestled on top of us, or your last day, when you made your way to the cool shade of the mulberry tree. We still imagine you there, and in the doorways, a black and white blur, in and out and out and in and now out forever.

Ellen Estilai

# Within the Margin of Error

The Woman Who Kept Her Own Counsel lived in a long narrow house just within the Margin of Error. Hers was the only house on the only street within the Margin of Error, which itself was nestled in a tiny, dark, impassable divide between two towering mountains. To the east of the Margin of Error, the steep terrain was densely wooded. To the west, it was rocky and desolate.

The long, narrow house within the Margin of Error—a kind of railroad flat--was cheap, because so few were willing to spend any time there. The mountain dwellers on either side regarded the Margin of Error with fear and distrust, if they regarded it at all. They feared and distrusted each other even more. But they thought the Woman Who Kept Her Own Counsel was mysterious. They didn't understand her, but they gave her the benefit of the doubt. She is neither here nor there, they said, neither fish nor fowl, neither plus nor minus. She is not one of us.

The mountain dwellers were populations of interest, but not to the Woman Who Kept Her Own Counsel.

Many before her had tried to live within the Margin of Error, but only the Woman Who Kept Her Own Counsel had succeeded. She had become adept at uncertainty. In fact, after half a century of living within the Margin of Error, she had come to understand that uncertainty was crucial to her existence. That knowledge was the only thing of which she was certain.

The Margin of Error varied from day to day, and the house and its divide expanded and contracted to accommodate it. The house's width was linked somehow to the contentiousness of the neighboring mountain dwellers and to the number of their voices. The fewer of them who chattered and nattered, the wider the Margin of Error became. If more of them filled their lungs and bellowed across the divide, the Margin of Error narrowed. Sometimes there was so much noise, the Woman Who Kept Her Own Counsel had to walk sideways.

The Woman Who Kept Her Own Counsel had learned to live within these margins--sometimes narrow, sometimes wide, but rarely comfortable. A house within the Margin of Error was hard to furnish, for one thing. One never knew whether to buy the six-inch sauté pan or the 16-inch wok, a side-by-side refrigerator or an ice chest, a box grater or a micro plane, a wide-brimmed sun hat or a skullcap. Her furniture was collapsible, her life accordion-folded.

Yet the Woman Who Kept Her Own Counsel never complained. Despite, the uncertainty, she liked the privacy. Hardly anyone paid attention to her. The mountain folk had no idea what the Margin of Error was or even how it got there, or why it was wider at times than at others. All they knew was that until the Margin of Error disappeared, there would be doubts.

For half a century, the Woman Who Kept Her Own Counsel never ventured outside the Margin of Error. At night, she would lie in her string hammock, her arms folded on her bony chest, her spine just inches from the divide below her floorboards, and try to imagine what it was like outside the Margin of Error. She could hear her mountain neighbors' raucous voices overhead, random samplings of their fears and suspicions echoing back and forth across the Margin of Error, bouncing off rock outcroppings and disappearing into eagles' nests and insinuating themselves into gopher holes, as the walls of her narrow house closed in on her, then retreated, then closed in again.

Then one day, the voices stopped. Unaccustomed to silence, the Woman Who Kept Her Own Counsel listened carefully for her neighbors' echoes, but the Margin of Error was still, except for the wind blowing through the empty space between the mountains. The Woman Who Kept Her Own Counsel climbed into her hammock, folded her arms across her bony chest and waited for the neighbors to resume their debates. But the only sounds she heard were a scraping as the walls of her house inched closer together, and a creaking as the floorboards buckled, and a crunch as the hammock collapsed into the divide, until finally, there was no room for error.

Nan Friedley

# being second

means you rarely wear shirts
not yet *broken in*
or play with toys that still
have price tags on them

your older brother set the bar
for comparison
are you taller, smarter, more athletic
parents, teachers, neighbors
watch you forge your way

you've never known what it's like
not to share
wait your turn
follow in bigger footsteps

your baby photo album
pictures loosely
tossed in a box

when you're second
parents don't dote on you
like your big brother
leaving you independent
discover what makes you special

I understand
I'm a second

Nan Friedley

# Hand Me Downs

It still had that new car smell and only 17 miles on the odometer.

It was the first car that hadn't been passed down to me from a grandpa or mother-in-law or driven to death by two brother-in-laws before me.

It scrutinized me on the lot with its jumbo headlights and seduced me with its grinning grille to take a test drive. It was *love at first sight*…a 1975 jelly bean yellow AMC Pacer with a wide body and greenhouse-like windows.

It was mocked by many but I loved it. Together we survived the Blizzard of '76 without jumper cables, threaded a 15-car pile up in whiteout conditions and dodged on-coming cars on Interstate 69's black ice. We were invincible, like Batman and Robin.

It was a few years later that my father-in-law was given a new company car and decided that I should inherit his practical, dull blue Chevy Citation and sell my quirky Pacer. I was devastated.

It was "an offer I couldn't refuse" coming from the patriarch of our Irish Catholic family.

It had 31,486 on the odometer and smelled like him.

Nan Friedley

# I Read the Obituaries

not every day
not every one
but feel I owe them a
few minutes of my time

some list every school and
every city they lived in and
every job they had and
every hobby they enjoyed and
every church they attended

always mentioned are those
who remain to feel the loss
a loving spouse, children,
grandchildren, and great grandchildren
who may only know them through old
sepia photos with scribbled names
dates on the back

will they have a tombstone
in a family plot of matching stones
or be released in the wind
cremated dust

is there a black and white photo
in a medaled uniform
or one more recently taken
with eyes that say *I'm ready*

Nan Friedley

# In the Center of the House

at the top of the stairs
to the right
was her only bathroom
in the house at Harlansburg

if I had been the porcelain
claw foot tub
I could tell tales of a
thresherman's wife
daughter of a Civil War vet
soaking in the soap's
ash and lye film

if I had been the porcelain
claw foot tub
I could tell tales of an
accountant's wife
survivor of the depression
lounging in lavender scent
listening to melodies
of backyard birds
through the window's screen
wishing she were somewhere else

if I had been the porcelain
claw foot tub
I could tell tales of a
young girl holding tightly
certain the bath would take a stroll

with her as an unwilling passenger

tugging
rubber stopper on a metal chain
blug, blug, blug
water drains
remnants of what was
Harlansburg, Indiana

Nan Friedley

# The Last Farmer

rented the farmhouse
parceled the land
sold tractors and his legacy
in auction
highest bidder
bought remnants
of a family business

the farmer before him
said there's nothing for you
here
acres of land portioned
profits divided too many ways
carve a new path for yourself

the farmer before him
gave his sons no choice
increased acreage
more livestock
their destiny was determined
a family empire at stake

the farmer before him
started it all
after the Civil War
a few acres
some cattle
faith

Nan Friedley

# Violated

privacy pried open, bent
left exposed
key useless now
outgoing mailbox breached
15 in all
 mine #10

you ravaged
six on the left
my flimsy door
dented, scratched
this time

that barking dog by the fence
a late-night jogger
must have stopped you
snatching
my social security check
20 bucks in a birthday card

thought I had dodged
invasion
but you returned
to dismantle
my fragile lock
broken pieces
left to taunt me
your screwdriver
picked my identity

life's secret numbers

saw your photo in the press
page 3, the local section
at least I hope it was you
stamped for delivery
to federal court

Nan Friedley

# You Want a Piece of Me?

Inspiration from Tedd Arnold of Parts, More Parts, and Even More Parts

It was Senior Day at Food for Less and I was armed to the teeth with coupons and recycle bags to take a bite out of the 10 % discount. The store is in a dicey neighborhood, but I was ready to kick some serious butt if necessary. As usual, there was a cart adjacent to my parking spot, actually in my parking spot. What a pain in the neck.

As a rule of thumb, I check the weekly flyer for the best bargains. Lately, I've been having a sweet tooth so the box of Frosted Flakes on the top shelf should appease my craving. I just couldn't reach it. A tall gangly guy was passing by so I asked him if he could give me a hand. He said, "Sure, it was no skin off his nose" and winked at me. I was tongue tied. He looked familiar but I couldn't put my finger on where I knew him from.

Standing in the checkout, I shuffled through my coupons hoping I didn't have to pay an arm and a leg. The cashier told me I had saved $43.25. That was a load off my mind. As I'm dumping bags into my trunk the tall gangly guy appeared.

"Give me your bags, lady."

"Over my dead body;" I replied. "I'll scream my lungs out and all eyes will be on you."

"Don't give me any lip."

I pleaded with him to have a heart.

It was then that a Security Cop saved my gluteus maximus.

Now I remember where I know him from. He was

a blind date I'd had decades ago. I wish I'd have given him a knuckle sandwich then.

    I went to pieces laughing my head off as the flat foot cuffed the guy. Time to face the music.

Alexis Gonzalez

# Hope is

Hope is a bright
Orb of light buzzing
Within our bellies
A tapestry of woven feelings
As uncontainable
As air.
We breathe.

It is a moment
It is a feeling of life
Revealing
A kind of love that lifts
Tired feet
Above the ceiling.

Hope is a bright
Orb of light
Let go of fighting the waves
of life
Succumb to light
Let it bring you to shore
It works every time
Of this I'm sure.

Alexis Gonzalez

# Winter

Cycles of seasons,
They must have their reasons.
No cold of winter,
Can last forever.
So I wait for spring,
My next endeavor.

Alexis Gonzalez

# Light and Dark

Sunlight
casting violet shadows
Over snowcapped peaks.
Moonlight
Casting violent shadows
Over ice cold feet.

The light always comes,
As so it leaves.

Alexis Gonzalez

# Once I Get There

I dart between the buildings,
The clock tower
It rings
I hear the night
And the beautiful ways it sings.

As I take flight
Among the sparkling
sapphire sky,
I hear the whisper of humans
As I fly on by.

My wings
they move
my wings
they fly
I propel myself
Way up into the sky.

I have no troubles
I just don't care
I'll find what I need
Once I get there.
Where?
Anywhere.

I dart between the buildings,
The clock tower
It rings

I hear the night
And the beautiful ways it sings

Judy Kohnen

# Bugged

An insect swam in the
bottom of the stainless
steel dog bowl, circling,
frantic to find footing
in millimeters of water.

Ugly is its creepy little vest
of articulated armor,
rolled like a feather parker,
Cockroach, earwig or beetle
I've no desire for inspection
—only feelings of burden,
frustration drowning in
a treadmill of chores
the politics of the day
and all the things
I cannot fix

I overturn the bowl
watch little legs
scratch the clouds
until the flip, and the tuck,
of its battered carapace,
and a slow drag to
higher ground.

Judy Conibear Kohnen

# I took the world for a walk today

I took the world for a walk today.
The wind was cold on my cheeks
it stung inside my nostrils when
I felt something strange
like an ejaculation between my thighs.
On top of my shadow I found
a puddle of primordial slime.
"Disgusting," said the scientist
as he sidestepped the fluids,
"germs are spread by saliva."

I kept walking, queasy,
things inside me were
loose and unmoored
I squeezed my cervix
and my thighs together
but a lime-green pod squirted
past my lady lips, shooting forth
eager to kiss the ground below.
It had a root bulb with hairs
like an onion, and inside
an embryonic eye stared
  upwards to heaven.

"It's a mermaid's purse!"
exclaimed a little girl,
skipping on the beach.
She took it home happy
to show it to her parents.

I kept walking. A snake
slid out of my vagina.
It slithered down my leg.
"That's an abomination,"
people scolded. They
made me feel uncomfortable
so I shed my skin until I was
smooth and virginal.

The apple came next.
It got bruised when it
dropped to the ground.
A handsome man picked it up
and he ate the apple. He
thought it tasted sinfully delicious.

The worst pain was the marble pillar.
Hard and cold, it ripped
stretched my perineum
as its Corinthian crown
breeched and protruded.
I stood rooted upright as
it lifted me off my feet
it grew and grew
until I was a dainty angel,
perched on top.
Tribesmen tried to knock me off
shaking the foundations, chanting.
I slid down the fluted pole and fled
before the tower came crashing down.

That was not my most magnificent delivery
—a castle thumped out, victorious like a lusty hero.
I felt proud as any king and marched
with a mighty song in my step.

The crowds cheered and bowed
as I dropped crenellations,
domes and temples
jettisoning them like
fortified earthquakes rippling the planet.

But thereafter, I dropped only slums,
sprawling slums that bled me out,
discharging with my placenta.
You people were yelling at me
I was confused about the reason,
an abortion or miscarriage,
that's when I ran away from home.

First I went into the closet
to find a leash for the world.
Seems like a long time ago
whispered breath of time
when I was once like you are now.
My ovaries are withered seeds.
They too, have fallen out.
I buried them deep in sweet moist earth,
but they are sterile. My
body follows their descent,
my decline tumbles into an arid landscape,
leaving a plume of stardust for you
to inhale on a cold, bitter day.

Marvin G. Meyer

# Cooking on an Oklahoma Farm, 1920

I was born in early 1936 on a farm that had no electricity. I am sure this affected my mom's cooking as we had no refrigeration, only an "Ice Box." We grew veggies which my mom, Lena Sawatzky Meyer, canned for our winter food supply. We also sometimes butchered a beef and a pig at the same time; this procedure allowed us to mix the hamburger and ground pork together. Butchering day was a very long and busy day. We kids did not go to school on this day, as all hands were needed. The mixed ground meat was very juicy and tasted great. Beef roast was cut in chunks and canned for later use.

When we butchered a pig, the fat was put through a grinder and then placed in a large 30-inch diameter kettle and rendered, or cooked. About a gallon of cracklins' were screened from this liquid lard. These were different than the pork skin cracklins' sold today. Not only did we eat them for breakfast, they were in great demand by our relatives. They were very fatty but because we worked so hard, it did not seem to cause a problem with our weight. Ribs were also cooked in the rendering pot. They were a treat that was often our lunch on butchering day. While all this butchering was going on, someone was very diligently cleaning the animals' intestines as they were used as sausage casings.

At some point, a commercial walk-in freezer was built in Clinton, a town seven miles from our farm. This innovation was a great improvement as we rented a chest there and preserved our meat in it. We almost always went into town on Saturday. On the way home, we picked up ice for our icebox and mom's weekly supply of frozen beef or pork from our supply. This was a task we did very quickly as it was zero degrees in the freezer room. We also grew and ate a great deal of frying chickens. This sounds easy, but it was a much larger task than it is today. We had to catch the bird, kill it, scald off the feathers, singe off the fine hair, cut it up into pieces, and finally cook it!

I have not talked much about mom's cooking but more about how much work it was for her to cook. I do remember what she packed in my school lunch for my first day at a one-room country schoolhouse. It was good and I was not done yet when lunchtime was over. I just stayed on the front porch of the school until I finished.

Around the 1940's, rural electrification came to our farm. This improvement was a big thing! Suddenly we had lights, refrigerators, and power for many tasks and cooking became easier for my mom.

Although she was German, her people lived in the Ukraine area of Russia for over 100 years so that culture may have influenced some of her recipes. She cooked some very delicious rolls called "twibucks" as in "ein, twi, dri"… These were two-story rolls with a large bottom and a smaller top. We liked to dismantle them, punch in a hole, pour it full of syrup and eat it. She also made a cottage cheese dumpling they called "varenicus" which was cooked in water. All of mom's cooking was good and I do not remember ever not having enough food—except when she made chocolate pudding. There was only enough for one very small dessert bowl for each of us. I can still taste how good that little bowl of pudding was. I wonder, would I remember that pudding so well if I had been able to get all I wanted?

Later, when we were living in town, mom would make cinnamon rolls that were delicious. Although I think she was already fighting cancer, she would occasionally bake these homemade rolls for a friend and me. I think she liked me! I could not have had a better mom or cook. I have now lived almost twice as long as she did.

Marvin G. Meyer

# Mischief at a Country Church, 1920

Mischievous pranks can be a lot of fun; however, they can also be disastrous. As I was growing up in Western Oklahoma, my mom, Lena Meyer, told me of a prank that her brother, Henry Sawatzky, and his friend pulled.

The setting was a Mennonite Church several miles out in the country from Corn, Oklahoma. Corn is a small German village about two blocks by three blocks in size. I spent much of my time at the church where my family worshipped. During the evening services, it was normal, as babies fell asleep, for their moms to carry them out of the church and put them in their horse-drawn wagon or buggy. There were not many cars in those days and people were not worried about crime. After all the babies were out and the moms were back, Uncle Henry and his friend slipped out of the service and began their little joke. They picked a baby out of a wagon, carried it to the next wagon, deposited the baby there, took the one belonging to that wagon to the next and so on.

When the service was over and the families came out in the dark, they did not notice that they had someone else's baby in the wagon. They just told the horses to "giddy-up" and they headed home to their farms some miles away. As there were no telephones, it took weeks to get the babies back to their proper families. Each mother cared for the child she had until she found its mother. Apparently no child needed any special medicine or needs as I was never told that the prank resulted in any disaster or damage.

Kimmery Moss

# Appetite

How many wants equal a life?

Do you run through them quickly
Burn your cash
Get, get, get
Or move it slow, instead
      Every sip of tea tasted
            Every sunset savored
                  Every love leaned into

Your want in your back pocket
Your heart up front

Kimmery Moss

# Eventuality

Tonight, you called
Though you are removed
By you
Sometimes I think
I may have done it myself,
Had I had
The courage.

To me,
You will always be me
You the survivor
You the solver of problems
You the dark man
With the turquoise eyes
So blue

And then you said it to me
After my wedding
About a man who looks like you
But is not you

In one sentence,
In the front seat of my car

Torn open again
I seep,
Everywhere.

Heart taut

Taught not to trust

I carry that with me.

And now you are gone again
But sometimes you call
And I always pick up.

Kimmery Moss

## Invertebrate

Velvety, delicate tissue
Beneath bony, calcified spokes

A body of violence
Crashed by tides
Suffocation and sun
Arms removed by curious toddlers,
Aquatic carnivores

Regrowing
Habitually
After each assault

No fish can manage this
A soul of constant rebirth
The star of the sea
A beach pea
Precious debris
Resiliency

Kimmery Moss

# Nirvana

Awakened
In the morning
In the monastery
Asleep again, under starry skies.

How many times?
How many times, he asks
He waits for his answer
He waits to wake again.

Kimmery Moss

# Tied Together

*Oh and by the way—*
You interject into the buzz of the web
    *I'm wearing a grey tie with a flower like, design on it*

I read your electronic note and smirk
because you punctuated clumsily

You speak with me in this secret language
we've somehow created
with our lips and our limbs and hearts
where commas don't matter.

I'm coming to find
that only a few things do:
Where I belong
What color the sunrise is in the east
and what makes birds sing every morning

You teach me about the little things
Like sea glass on the shore
And kisses on the neck
And what you wore today

*It's a funky tie,*
you say.
*I dig it.*

Cindi Neisinger

# Evolution of the Mission Inn: Her View

Pre-Riverside the land belonged to Mexico.

Soon colonies were formed around me,
land and irrigation brings my family.
Millers arrive,
purchase a block,
built a home called Glenwood,
soon to change to a family business.

Frank Miller, their son, at 23
buys Glenwood Hotel from his dad,
takes a bride
named Isabella

Now Oranges are the rage.
Bringing in wealth, investments and tourists.
Buildings start to spring up around me.

My name changes.
The Mission Inn is evolving.
Mission wing, with it's court of birds.
Two funny macaws named Napoleon and Joseph fly about,
and make me laugh.
Cloister wing and Catacombs!
Yes! They exist....
Spanish wing with its art gallery,
and more!
Rotunda Wing, and romantic chapel.

My friend Frank Miller dies. I am sad.
But, not his vision.
His children and grandchildren,
try to keep it going
till they pass too.

I feel lost.
The new owner modernizes.
However, business becomes lackluster.
Yet another investor tries too.
A dark time indeed.
Bankruptcy probability.
Uncertainty ….

Now at last! A glimmer of hope,
my knight in shining armor appears
and
saves me.
Frank's dreams are realized through him.

The city rallies to my side!
A parking lot I won't become.
A National Historic Landmark
Hotel is now my title.
Which I wear proudly.
Guarded by my friends and docents,
Never to be torn down.

The Keepers of the Inn
are my heroes.
All my history and art is protected.

Lots of movies were made here.
Ten Presidents have visited,
I even have a big chair President Taft sat in.
Ask about the circus elephant that ran amuck?

Through a long history of ups and downs.
I have endured.

I do…
Weddings, they are my niche.

The Festival of Lights
is a dazzling spectacle.
Four million-plus lights decorate me.

Come see me for yourselves, and take a tour.
I'm not going anywhere……

Gary Neuharth

# Creation

Electrons convulsed within the cauldron of creation
    and molecules shook as neon gasses of brilliant green
        spun down lazily into infinity from creation itself.

The great act had begun from within the purple clouds
    of exploding dwarf stars.
        It seemed to cover the vastness of it all
            and multicolored stars seemed to wane
                in the vacuum of airless anticipation.

The great funnel of Orion spun outward in one majestic movement
    like a spiral of unimaginable force lazily hurling planets out into
        the great void where each world from this star factory
        sped noiselessly on its own random voyage
            into the crystal clarity of the great starry void.

Out of the void of the exploding funnel
    came a great noiseless shout
        from the unseen presence
            that suddenly awakened.

It needed no name to announce itself
    for every intelligence that existed
        heard the noiseless declaration
            and rocked to the feeling of its power.

The Father of everything that ever existed had called out to them
    and every mother's child turned
        to feel their outer covering stripped away

and countless dancing electrons pulsated
    transforming back into their simplest forms –
        naked pulsing bursts of light.

Gary Neuharth

# I Love

It was suspended laying in a sea of memories of a young boy in a white house
The smell of walnut trees and the aroma of chicken soup
The large white-haired fading blond with big breasts and big arms
And Father – he was there
But his mother was my mother most of the time –
She was always there in the two-story white house
      under the mother of magnolia trees
Outside was surrounded by the lowliness of the small white picket fence
The smell of motor oil hung in the air
And the dust in the driveway gave the aroma of ancient dust
      and the mystery of the old pump house
Almond trees hung like sentinels around the edges
      with their own particular smells
So many smells –
      rotting grapes and hot cement
      and irrigation ditch with the clean smell of water and mud mixing
All those odors and the cool gurgling waters trail in the rich black muddy rows.

The barn was so big –
      huge machines and the heavy smell of grease
      and the heavy layers of dust collecting
It was a beautiful world – I love penetrated everything

I was so in love with everything

    like the old board steps to the water tower behind the
garage
     a secret room at the top with years of untouched dust
     inside lay unyielding behind a rusty door
     time lay unmoving in that room
     and through the slats in the walls
       sunlight shone in shafts of white light in the
swirling dust

I could lay on the floor and dream in that room
I could close my eyes and listen and dream
I don't remember ever leaving – but I did
I remember returning
    I was bigger – 20 years bigger
     and the two-story house with a basement was very
small
    everything was so much less – so little
That feeling of love – it was smaller too
Maybe it was love that had made it all so large and beautiful
My first dreams were fading and my first love was shrinking
I love – had run away with me into the neon sky and the sun's
re-orange eye

Sometimes when you stood in the shade of the walnut trees
    you could hear the echoes of voices –
    voices from the past where love grew on a summer
day
    like a rainbow glowing magically at noonday.

Gary Neuharth

# I Remember

I remember the tall night sky and the clear blue sky and a small cat's eyes
I remember small boys in sailor suits standing transfixed against white stucco walls
I remember milk bottles falling out of the sky at noon day and splintering glass
I remember my first kaleidoscope and the swirling prisms and colored stars transposing
      with a turn of my wrist. My dull world would vanish away and I would glide inside
      a paper pipe parallel to spectrums of changing colors bright and luminous.
I remember the naked girl that ran shrieking through the corn field and no one chased
      her or followed her or hunted her. She was alone.
I remember the headlines on the newspaper declaring Hitler's call
I remember two thousand faces reflecting Adolph's iron hand
I remember climbing steep hills shaped like giant fingers pointed skyward
I remember following people, tall silent ones who rarely spoke
I remember trains and boxcars and train tracks and twilight rumbling
I remember sleeping in a boarded shack by the tracks on a cold night
I remember looking for glory in my pride and independence and there was none
I remember fat ladies at church with serpent tongues, hissing and swaying

I remember cold nights on a motorcycle in alleys on a one-way street
 I remember Main Street, old hotels, obnoxious smells of decaying garbage and people
I remember gathering in a dark room with platonic priests waiting
I remember cold light jail room cells and kindred souls
      It wasn't good to be beautiful inside wise-men undressing your mind
I remember grand visions of floating piano keys and floating faces and enchanting
      music that came from gold barrages in sewer tunnels
I remember the little girl from Brooklyn and her face changing to the North
I remember riding with hitters on the freeway through Camarillo
      I always woke up in fields of shopping carts and tall waving grass
I remember long walks with long strides in the dawns gleaming
I remember roses, the roses seemed to be following my steps
I remember the dark-haired wise-woman with rainbows inside of her
I remember New Orleans and silent screams and words walking
I remember love in women's eyes and my desperate yearnings, too much desperation,
      disattachment and their following me around.
It was easy, too easy now, even though it was what I wanted before.

"More spirit," they kept calling, maybe it was because they had none.
Drummers on the boardwalk with their dark mating call.
Revelations, consummations, inspiration calling for security.
Reflections on the ocean waves, hands lifted in the summer clouds.
Toilet paper figures dressed in shrouds and a girl in bird land.
I remember voices calling, "Hey, little old man" and I wasn't old.
I remember girls slouching dressed in innocent white robes
I remember 2 steps forward and taking 3 steps backward
I remember feeling guilty remembering my past.
I remember the beginning of winter and the frost of indifference.
The cold seems to show every thought now, will summer ever come?
The hunt for open headed smiling faces is now a secondary thought.
I remember being good and feeling bad about it later
I remember Snow White on roller skates being pummeled with strawberries.
I remember Cleveland, 3 choir boys salivating and a half-step on a clarinet
I remember utopia blooming in the land of the red man and closing again
I remember baby's blue eyes, blue as sapphires and clear as glass
I remember 200 tambourine players in Fairmont Park,
Thousands of tiny bells and wrists shaking with no conductor
I remember the paranoid piano player scared and playing a beautiful minuet
I remember dances in coffee houses unpretentious and unpredictable

I remember black door bars and little people with wings dancing
I remember a drummer inseparable to the drum using no sticks,
      riveted to the skin instinctively predestined prettily.
There's a mouse with suspenders who stands on the rim.
      He says, "I like to know you but I can't let you in."
      So, you stand outside trying to remember.

But now it's all very clear. It was not the mouse at all.
Now it comes flooding back in a sea of memories.
The store master is running and the once powerful bear is afraid
The closet girl has stage fright and the Amazon turns away.

I remember it all!
The tall buildings – the trains – the field of waving grain – the high sky
I remember past – and present – and I see you – and I remember you
All of you

Gary Neuharth

## The Boat

And lo
It was night
And I began to dream.

I was in a great ocean. Its waters had once been clean and clear as glass.
And its name was called The Sea of Purity.
Now, it was muddy and called The Sea of Indifference.

A boat was slowly making its way across. On its bow was the name "The Pursuit of Happiness."
In the boat was a fat man. He was wearing golden robes and his pockets were full of gold.
He wore a wide brimmed hat with the words "Personal Interest" clearly written on its band.
His name was Bureaucrat.
He was paddling the boat with two large oars with the words POWER TO THE PEOPLE written on them.
The words had mostly worn off now and all that could be clearly seen was the word POWER.
The boat had a beautiful sail called "The Constitution" but it was rolled up tightly and bound with amendments.

I was in The Sea of Indifference with thousands of others struggling to keep our heads above the waters. The fat man in the boat saw us but continued to row and offered us no help.

There were two cities on opposite sides of the shoreline.
One city was called Fairness. Its main street was called

Equality.
The other city was called The Evolution of Power and its main street was called Intolerance.

We were all struggling in the sea calling out for help but the boat would not stop.
The land we so desperately wished for was too far away.

I awoke from my dream with a start.

Jane O'Shields-Hayner

# The Light From Our Steps

The light from our steps shined on the morning,
slicing the long net of nightmares and fear.
The reins of our future were laced through our fingers,
without mounts or weapons, our pathway was clear.

I stepped in the wave, keeping time with the marchers;
a blind woman swept the ground with her cane.
Babies and fathers, wheelchairs and banners
moved with the swell, and walked without shame.

Treading their paths, we honored our foremothers,
our past and our future both danced in the sun.
With righteous anger, we broke the locks open.
Set free from illusion, in grace we were one.

No fear overtook us. No evil befell us.
Through the street filled with marchers, I glimpsed the white cane.
Our streets were our oceans, our bodies our rivers,
our words became groundwater, calling our names.

The world owns the memories of the morning we shared,
when three million marchers stretched over the earth.
When power and love awoke with the sunrise,
with truth as our story, and courage our worth.

*The Light From Our Steps* was published in Lady Liberty Lit on January 28, 2017. Jane wrote it after participating with her family in The Women's March, held January 21, 2017. She was enrolled in Stephanie Barbe Hammer's online Poetry Class at the time and submitted it for review among her classmates.

Jane O'Shields-Hayner

# The Obsidian Mare

Obsidian black was the light she shone,
reflected from wind-ruffled mane and tail,
head raised, eyes set, crossing prairies alone,
nimble, sure-footed, hooves high on the trail.
There was no another mount that could race her.
No ribbon lay torn before her dark breast.
Without a saddle, a bridle or quirt,
with black body low, she stretched long for the test.
The child lay upon her warm body, strong,
the bare-backed, shining, obsidian mare,
and flew like a crow without its own song
that sang through the flight of wind through her hair.
Fire always burns in the heart where love sings.
It flies like a black-bird through the long night,
carrying twigs, with brittle tips flaming,
in penance for longing and loving and flight.

The Obsidian Mare was published in Tiferet Journal, Winter edition, 2017. Jane wrote this poem while enrolled in an online poetry class with Stephanie Barbe Hammer and submitted it to the class for review.

Jeanne'marie Parsons

# Am I Destined to be a Cat Lady?

So here's my online dating profile - for real. And bare with me it's kind of long: I am 51 years young and a widow of almost 2 years. I am genuine, easy going, calm, affectionate, have a great sense of humor and tend to be more of an introvert in a non-reclusive way. I am flirtatious in the quiet sense and affectionate in the sensual sense. I am liberal to middle of the road and agnostic but also spiritual. I am healthy and fit but not to the extreme. I enjoy the outdoors (a bit of jogging, walking, tennis and hiking). I love most types of music (blues rock, alternative, soul, Motown and admit to being a pop junky but I won't subject you to it :) and not much for twangy country). I love to travel -weekend getaways and vacations (just went to Spain). I do enjoy going out (dinner, coffee, theatre, concerts) but really prefer more quiet, calm intimate venues and settings which is why I probably favor good take out and kicking back with someone in the comfort of home. If you are drama free, humble, easy going, respectful, spiritual (just not an extreme religious fanatic), healthy (but not a gym junky), independent (holding your own), love to laugh and have a great quiet (somewhat sarcastic) sense of humor, and are a bit of an introvert yourself, we might be a good match.

I don't think that's asking for much, right? Ok, yeah it's a lot.s But I'm not asking for the Mercedes or the Ferrari. I'm not asking for the mansion on the hill or the amazing tropical paradise vacation. I'm not asking for financial statements to prove your valid existence of being. I'm not asking for drop dead Bradley Cooper out of my league gorgeous. And I'm not asking for the knight in fucking shining armor to sweep me off my feet. Grant it, there are a few key criteria that must be met, i.e. a nongregarious liberal thinker who has somewhat the same political and religious views as myself - which I think are valid issues. But other than that, I'm just asking for what I would think most human beings would be - an independent, nice, calm, simple, drama free, respectful guy. So where the fuck are they?

Here's what I've gotten:

PG guy: "So do you have any drama in your life?" "No, just my ex pregnant on and off girlfriend." "Ha ha! That's a joke right?" "No, she really is my on and off pregnant girlfriend. But she won't know."

Drop off text guy: "So I really want to meet you. Let's definitely get together tonight." "Cool. Ok. Where and what time?" "Oh, I'll text you later." ...Hours later. Two words: Radio. Silence.

No number guy: "So I really like you and want to keep chatting." "Ok. So why don't we exchange numbers so we can chat easier?" "Oh I don't want to do that. My wife might want to use it against me if we divorce."

No face guy: "So why don't you have a picture of your face on the site?" "Isn't the pic of my huge bare chest enough." "Well yeah, but it'd be nice to see your face - see what you look like. "Oh. So you're a prude then." Wtf?

Starving actor guy: "I'd love to meet. Let's meet halfway between LA and your place. But see I drive a BMW SUV and I don't make much acting. So I need you to pay for half of my gas." Really?

And then there's the multiple want to see my cock guys: "So I liked your profile and thought I'd message. How's your day going?" "Fine. Want to see my cock?"

Since when did, "Do you want to see my cock become a pick up line?" I know I'm of "mature" age, but really? Where are the nice, decent guys? Are they really all taken because they are the nice guys? I find that hard to believe because I'm a nice chick and it seems there must be good guys out there looking for the same thing.

I know it's possible because I found my late husband online and he was a really nice guy. This was years ago after I struggled with a 15 year first marriage. Similar to today, I was scrolling through my email of yahoo personals. I had just about given up the idea of online dating when I clicked on the message, "65Mopar is interested in you." What popped up was the kindest smile I had ever seen. This tall man standing in this meticulous office, his body framed by bookcases of perfection, later to find out categorized by the Dewey Decimal System. Wearing perfectly pressed Levi's and a green corduroy jacket with patched elbows, he looked every bit a professor which he was - professor and dean emeritus for a prominent school of Theology in So. Cal. He also loved vintage cars and had completely restored a beautiful 1965 Chrysler Belvedere. Hence the screen name "65Mopar." We emailed back and forth for a few months and finally decided to meet for coffee at a quaint corner cafe. I know this sounds silly and juvenile, but it was love at first sight. I remember him telling me that after leaving coffee that day, he professed to himself, "That's the woman I'm going to marry." That evening we met for drinks and never looked back.

We spent every day together for the next four years it seems, each day feeling like it was pure excitement like the first. We were married shortly after our four year courtship to which a year later he was diagnosed with terminal cancer. I quit my job and cared for him full time the next three and a half years and am grateful I did. As devastating as it was to lose him, I have no regrets. Because I have nothing but the fondest memories of him. And it is because of our relationship that I know I can find that happiness once again.

And so I sit here again at my laptop sifting through a plethora of male species interested in my undeniable sexy smile - so they proclaim. And yet nothing comes of it. It seems you get two extremes. At one end, they just wanna fuck. And at the other end, they want a lifelong commitment after two emails. What happened to good old lets just get to know each other first - be friends and see where it leads? It's a daunting and exhausting experience because it seems like an endless search of nothingness in a vast sea of testosterone. Why do I feel so pressed to find "the one" - again? And why does it seem so impossible?

Maybe we are so focused on looking for the exact perfect one, we can't clearly see around us. Is it a case of seeing the forest for the trees? I think so. We are so caught up in the obsession and panic of searching for perfection that we forget to look beyond what else is important. We exude desperation - an unattractive quality. I know. I have felt it. Because I never expected to be a widow so young and I don't enjoy being single. So yes, I'll admit it. I have felt desperate at times, Desperate to find a partner that I can be at peace with. Have a simple life with. Share companionship and just be my best friend.

And speaking of best friends and hopeless desperation? I have a best friend of over 30 years who is also recently single and deals with the same situations. The players and play are a little different, but still the same desperate drama to find peace and happiness that we all want. Her and I I continue to joke about moving in together one day, adopting 50 feral cats and growing old and shriveled while sitting on the front porch in our multi colored polyester moo moos. Is this what I am destined to become? A cat lady? I don't know. I mean - who really knows what our destiny will be except the certainty of our demise?

And so the search continues. Maybe cat lady - maybe not. Or maybe when I least expect it, that "one" will pass my way not knowing what hit me. Or just maybe when I'm sitting on that front porch rocking in my chair, one of those cats will magically turn into my knight in fucking shining armor and sweep me off my feet. Or maybe, I'll just grow old on that porch surrounded by cats, having a cup of tea with my best friend...after all.

Karl Pettway

# Intro to Reading

I was a late bloomer when it came to reading, writing, or the fundamentals of anything. I did pretty much as I was told but I wasn't told much. We moved from New York City to Detroit when I was around six years old. I had been briefly exposed to many cultures (Puerto Rican, Jewish, Gypsy, Irish…) which made me kind of a strange kid living in the very conservative Midwest. I was teased a lot and got in many fights, mostly because I talked funny. I needed glasses. My mother couldn't afford them. I was malnourished and homeless much of the time and so on. I guess it is a common situation for that place in time. I think I was more greatly affected because this happened during my formative years.

My early cross-cultural exposure fueled my ability to daydream about strange people in faraway lands. I was usually somber, but like a wilting plant or flower, I quickly livened up with just a little watering and attention. My way of coping was to develop a strong imagination. My reading repertoire consisted of *Mad Magazine*, sneaking a short peek at one of my aunt's trashy dime store novels, and comic books. Perhaps I could have been a great fiction writer like Stan Lee, H.G. Wells, or Rod Serling. I was interested in everything, just anything to allow my mind to escape the horror of my depressing environment.

Mrs. Summers, our elementary school English teacher, replaced traditional Dick and Jane books with the Farina and Buckwheat series, which featured unkempt, barefoot Black kids, who wore ragged clothes and spoke in an inferior form of broken English. She must have reasoned that to be appropriate in the Black classrooms. While my classmates giggled and laughed, I felt ashamed and degraded. I lost interest in scholastic reading until the third grade, when we got a substitute teacher named Miss Roberts. She had us select from an approved reading list from the school library. We shared our choices by writing about the characters and reading out loud to the class. I chose the book *Morgan the Pirate*. It took a long time for me to read the book because I didn't have a suitable reading environment at home. In the end, the book left thoughts of swashbucklers, scallywags, and skullduggery on the high seas.

    A few years ago the world seemed to catch up to my fascination with all things "pirate." The fashion merchandise industry has certainly cashed in on the old skull and crossbones—and, the sports world does have the Pittsburgh Pirates, Oakland Raiders, and Tampa Bay Buccaneers.

Karl Pettway

# Winter

Visiting the Midwest from Southern California is like time machine travel, especially in winter time. Many Detroit neighborhoods feature vacant lots overgrown with weeds. Central downtown areas are seeing a slow renaissance—but coming out to about 8 Mile Road is a disaster zone.

Few people can remember the City the way it was when I was a kid. Throughout the late 1950s, it was a vibrant cultural center, alive with industry, merchants, arts, and music. In the mid-1960s it turned into a ghost town overnight. Not much has changed since then. In the winter the daytime skies resemble a great flannel canopy. Greenery gives way to grey and black tree branches with snow-white ledges that linger all winter long. The film noir-like setting could be an Ansel Adams artwork.

People seem glad to see their neighbors as they scurry about in their tweed, wool, and furry garments. Winter nights can be even more beautiful than they are dangerous. Dark blue skies contrasted by snow covered roof and window ledges with pure white velvety blankets of snow create a fairytale-like setting. Night air is crisp and the colors are sharp and rich. Blues range from midnight, chromium, cobalt, Navy, Air Force, gun metal, aquamarine, to even periwinkle; and feel almost magical. It makes me think of "All Blues," or "Round Midnight," by Miles Davis.

Relationships between family and friends seem richer and deeper too. I talk to my nieces, nephews and friends at least once a week. Out west things are much different. People greet each other in a courteous, brief kind of way. Other than my brother, I haven't talked to any long-time acquaintances in years.

Western winters give us many more sights to see. There are often cool evening breezes and snow-capped mountains in the distance, usually against pastel colored skies. We get indescribably beautiful sunsets daily. Rolling green foothills are speckled with a bounty of wildflowers. As they push toward the meadow beyond, they display even more wildflowers.

Gas prices are lower which could mean more trips to the beach. Beaches in the winter feature white capped waves and fewer distractions, especially near Palisades and Malibu.

Yes, I do like my winters out west the best.

Karl Pettway

# My First Car

My first car was a psychedelic metal flaked green, 1964 VW Bug. It had very thin florescent orange accent stripes. I put wider tires on and it was super cute. The year was 1969 so it was fairly new. My father drove off and left me at the auto dealer. I remember thinking – *no problem.*

Pop had taught me to how to drive at a very young age and, like most teens, I thought I knew just about everything. The problem was that it was a standard (stick) shift transmission. So, shifting gears and smooth clutching was going to take a little getting used to. It was a good thing that we lived only a couple of miles from the dealer. Scraping the gears, I eased down the back streets jerking on the shifter. At first I was a little embarrassed as the car shook and shimmied as I sputtered and bounced along. But by the time I got home I was driving like a pro.

I pulled up to the house and my Pop was just standing on the front porch with a big grin on his face. Without saying a word, his expression showed both pride because I had mastered it and resolve because he had taught that young know-it-all yet another lesson.

Karl Pettway

# Keepsakes

A lesson from community colleges that transferred on to universities is, "Keep stuff!" It had been a regular routine for me to eagerly sell my books at the end of every semester for 10 to 30 percent during the "buy back" programs. Immediately after finals I could hardly wait to collect the extra cash.

I started looking forward to visiting Mr. Green, a career counselor, at Cypress College in the late 1980s. He was a silver haired, older pipe-smoking white gentleman. His life seemed to be at the opposite end of the spectrum from mine. His office was filled with keepsakes, such as masks, emblems, statuettes, figurines, and assorted souvenirs from a lifetime of world travels—something I have always longed to do. Though we had practically nothing in common, he somehow represented what had been missing in my life. When administrators tried to schedule me to see any other counselor, I would say no. I'll wait for an appointment to see him. His globetrotting lifestyle made him just the kind of person I am drawn to. I wanted to be like him. I paid attention to the way he dressed; low keyed, downplayed and understated. I was young and flamboyant in those days. I usually wore silks, suede, leather, and lots of jewelry.

It was the 80s and I was missing the road leading to a meaningful life. I felt like the good things were sliding pass me. So I started noticing things about Mr. Green—like the way he dressed. He wore plain, comfortable, round toed shoes; soft colored woolen pants with a modest tie and tweed sports coat. This was a look that I didn't adhere to right away. My observations were not covert. He knew I wanted to know about everything. We discussed how, at age 35, I could convert into the kind of person I ought to be. It was more than just his appearance. I took into account his counseling skills too. We talked about many things, from pipes and aromatic tobaccos, to which majors I should choose.

I was about to transfer to a university and everything he advised me on, he supported by directing me to books from his collection for confirmation. Three particular pieces of advice that stick with me to this day are: do not sell back your books; keep all relevant coursework; and, stay in school for as long as you possibly can. Make them kick you out.

My formal education has been temporarily interrupted due to a lifetime of off and on homelessness. Meanwhile, I do little artwork projects and have been attending foreign language and writing workshops to keep busy and work on my social skills. Enduringly though, I have managed to hold onto my books and much of my coursework for over three decades. They are probably my greatest keepsakes –thank you Mr. Green!

Cindy Rinne

# Mother of All

*An apple a day.*

      That beautiful apple meant

woman messed up,

      crunch of juice,

seeds spread

      as Sheila suffered curse

of birth. Or did the goddess,

      Thesis, begin

the cosmos?

      Rosy apple tempted

Snowdrop,

      salty and sweet.

Half-poisoned skin,

      jealous Queen.

For Persephone,

  pomegranate seeds,

small and tart,

  just a few

for him to possess

  her underground

while the Earth's surface

  slept.

Kristine Ann Shell

# Catalina

It's the end of March. My sister, Karen, and her husband, Karl, are visiting from Texas. So, I'm in entertainment mode. My house has never been cleaner. Karen and Karl want to see Catalina Island while they're visiting us. Karen says she wants to visit Catalina before it gets too hot? I suspect she wants to visit during the off-season as everything's less expensive then. That's my sister!

It looks as though the weather will cooperate. The sun is shining and the temperatures are mild when we arrive in Avalon. We go for a walk along the beach. Check out the tourist traps. Check into our hotel. Many of the houses on the hills are painted in sunset colors. Blues, roses, yellows. Gas-powered vehicles that resemble golf carts zip up and down the streets. Thank heaven the weather is good.

When we wake the next morning, it's cloudy and the wind is cold. Oh well, one out of two days was nice. My husband, Bob, turns on the TV, local news and weather. Not good! There's a serious storm moving in. Bob heads to the Catalina Express ticket office to find out if Catalina Express is planning to change its schedule.

Bad news. The Catalina Express isn't guaranteeing any departures after 3 PM. The hotel we're staying at will be happy to extend our stay. But, how many days will we be in Catalina if we decide to stay past 3PM? And how much fun will we have cooped up in our rooms?

The wind has picked up. The air is colder. Large waves crash against the seawall. After talking with Karen and Karl, we decide to take the next ship out that has four open seats. We pack our things in a hurry and head for the docks. The ticket lines at the sea terminal are long and crowded.

I breathe a sigh of relief as we take our seats on the Express. The water's choppy. The ship rocks on the water. Karen and Karl take seats facing backwards. Karl says they're less likely to get seasick if they're looking backwards instead of forwards. My sister, Karen, tends to get seasick, so I go with it.

As the Express picks up speed, the ship's deck bounces and lurches on the water. The snack bar and the beverage bar are open, but few passengers seem interested. We're on the upper deck, Captains lounge. Two attendants serve complimentary drinks. Would a stiff drink help or hinder? Maybe a complimentary ginger-ale? The attendants balance their serving trays and move down the aisles like tightrope walkers. Many of the passengers have lowered the trays on the seats in front of them. Not for the complimentary drinks, but as places to lay their heads and the nausea builds. A big, bald man in uniform is handing out plastic barf bags. Not good.
My sister, Karen, isn't getting seasick. Maybe Karl was right about the seats. As we get closer to Long Beach, the clouds thin and the water calms. There are seagulls in the air. That must be a good sign. The ship slows as we pull into the harbor. The captain addresses passengers over the radio. He says he hopes the trip wasn't too stressful.

As we step off the ship and onto the shore, I consider kissing the solid ground beneath my feet. But, Karen is looking at me. So, I smile at her, and I say, "Well, that was fun!"

Kristine Ann Shell

# Taking a Gamble

Walk through any casino, and you'll find them: the lookers, the players, the gamblers. I'm mostly a looker - drawn to the casino's bright lights, special effects, party atmosphere. The clang and clatter of coins "paying off," the explosion of arcade music and lights, the console chairs that rival Disney's Star Wars attraction. Who wouldn't look? Pick a popular movie, fairy tale or fantasy. There's a slot machine for it.

Stay a short while, and you're an emerging player. Try the penny or nickel slot machines. But, beware the multiplier. A penny machine is not a penny if the multiplier starts at 25. I tell myself it's a lot like life. One risk or chance rarely breaks us. It's the multiplier that raises the stakes and wreaks havoc.

I trade $50.00 for a slip of paper. It's all I intend to risk. Did I say risk? I'm playing the slot machines. The house will take my money sooner or later. I play the slot machines for fun, not caring so much whether I win or lose. So, I shout when I win and groan when I lose. If I'm lucky, and every player believes in luck, I'll win a few games and have lunch at the buffet before I lose my $50.00.

The gamblers claim the table games. They play to win. They are focused, cool, calculating. They know the games, the odds, the cards, and they place their bets accordingly. Tobacco smoke clouds the air. Ashtrays overflow. Several players join the table games. They order drinks from the bar. The alcohol won't improve their games, but it may dull the pain of losing. Do some of the players consider themselves gamblers? Many will spend hours here under the artificial lights, breathing the smoke-filled air.

In a couple of hours, my $50.00 is gone. I take the

elevator to the casino's parking lot and head to my car. My eyes adjust to bright sunlight. A warm wind tosses my hair. I stop to watch the waterfall near the casino's entrance, and I know what's been said is true. Water flows to lower ground, but money moves in the opposite direction.

Kristine Ann Shell

# Mae Arrives

*A tribute to Mae Wagner Marinello, Writing Facilitator, Inlandia Institute*

Mae arrives,
unpacks her purse.
Candles, bluebirds,
Goldberg's works.

The conference room
is packed again.
Mae's students search
for chairs and pens.

Mae is here,
a writer's spring,
with prompts and clips,
and magazines.

A gentle heart,
a quiet ear,
a trusted friend,
Mae is here.

David Stone

# Standing Ground

"Birdie, birdie, birdie,"
calls the cardinal,
black masked, brilliant red.
"Purdy, purdy, purdy."
Crest-raised, alarmed,
the bird rattles its automatic
metallic "Chip, chip, chip, chip, chip.
Chip, chip, chip, chip chip,"
over the white-tailed deer.
"Whoit, whoit, whoit, whoit,"
he warns above the interloper's
dry nose, whose dangling head
silently drips frozen red
on the white snow.

David Stone

# Rest in the Grove

*for Benjamin Mileham Stone*

On the hill beyond the farm,
rest in the hickory grove
your forefather set aside
in hope of heaven's charm.

In the hollow the willows
weeping leaves will dry and sprout,
giving all sanctuary
along the water's endless way.

Stone stacked on stone will surround
you, a sentry standing more
than a century in wait
to move at the trump's last sound.

David Stone

# Hope

The light of morning
illuminates a ficus leaf,
green like Tiffany glass,
veins glowing yellow
over the crossed trunks
rising from an urn.

The light of morning
shines through a window,
Easter in an alcove,
while we wait
in the hospital's lobby
for Infectious Disease.

David Stone

# Two Hollows on a Hill

On a rock above the pond
where the two willows stand,
there's a dry dent ringed in dust
like a widowed lake after a drought.

A lone grain's husk haunts
the hollow where brown hands
knocked granite to granite and granite
to grain, two hundred years before
a white man made the pond.

David Stone

## At Last a Black Lily

I spied a raven in my yard,
not resting on a bust,
nor casting beady eye
or sounding throaty kraa,

but feathers fully splayed
as if a taxidermist's
hand had set his stance
fixed in sharpest pitch.

What disorientating pain
drove him to bury his head
fully as a root to leave
his wings a flower's petals?

At last, a black lily
floats on the Western Nile.

Gabrielle Symmes

# Losing Ginger

It was a Thursday, I think. I was busy running errands when I noticed the multiple missed calls, and text messages from my Dad. I must have forgotten to turn my ringer back on after my morning appointment. My Dad can be a little impatient at times, but this seemed different. I called him right away. The tone of his voice was panicked sounding. "I've been trying to reach you. Ginger's dead." The words flooded out of his mouth, as did the tears from his eyes. Through gulps and gasps, he finally came up with enough air to tell me that her neighbor had found her on the couch, in front of her T.V. set. Southern California Edison had arrived at her home that morning to work on power lines that crossed her back yard. Her front door was open, T.V. on, but the security screen was locked. They couldn't get anyone to answer their knocking, so that's when the self-proclaimed "nosey neighbor" sent her granddaughter to climb the fence and go around to the back door. From that vantage point, it was clear that something was very wrong, as Ginger was slumped over on the couch, and unresponsive to any of the pounding and shouting that the girl was doing at the back window and door.

The police and paramedics were called. An axe was used to get through the back door, but it was clear to them that she likely died the night before.

My Dad is her only sibling, and he lives far from his childhood family home in Rubidoux. The one that Ginger spent her entire 63 years living in. Over the phone, he tasked me with going to the Coroner's office in Hemet, and retrieving her keys, money, and I.D. The whole experience was surreal. Taking possession of the small bag of personal effects, driving to Rubidoux, and turning onto the street, Morey Way. I hadn't been in that house for over 20 years. Hardly anyone had. I turned the key and opened the front door. A wave of sadness hit me, followed by a wave of heat, and the smell of sixty plus years of pet ownership. How did I get here? She never would have let me through the door if she were alive. Always too embarrassed by her lack of housekeeping, followed by an intense desire for privacy. But here I was, staring at the couch where she lay dead just the day before. It was more than thirty years prior that I watched my frail Grandmother lie on a couch in this same living room, tethered to an oxygen tank, struggling for breath in her final days. Another wave of sadness nearly knocks me down. Lost years. Lost loved ones. Lost opportunities. With too much loss to reconcile and a job to be done, I shifted focus and began the task at hand. Assess the house, gather any valuables, and lock it up tight until my Dad arrives. Concerned friends and neighbors came knocking while I waded through empty cans of Diet Coke, and dust covered dreams.

In the weeks that followed, my Dad and his wife, Teresa, came to pick up the pieces, purge, and figure out how to move forward. It turns out there is a lot of business to dying. All of this while also figuring out how to honor Ginger and lay her to rest. I took on the responsibility of her Eulogy, arranging the service and reaching out to her friends. I went through the contacts on her phone and began calling and messaging, letting everyone who cared about her know that she was gone. I was never close with Ginger, and yet, I cried with each person I connected with and felt a deep sense of loss again and again.

My Dad's wife went through the house with the ferocity and expediency of a category five hurricane. She had multiple lifetimes of memories and mementos to go through in one month's time. The trash cans were filled and donation piles formed like a small mountain range in the driveway. My anxiety level went through the roof as I witnessed this. It felt like Ginger, and my family history, was being trashed, given away and lost forever.

    She was a saver, and accomplished artist, and a bit of an eccentric visionary. She had kept every birthday and Christmas card ever given to her by her parents and Grandmother, dating back to her first birthday and Christmas. This explained a lot. As an adult woman, Ginger preferred not to celebrate her birthday or Christmas. I think most of us thought her some kind of scrooge. As I laid hands on those cards and memories, her story unfolded, and it was that of a young girl and young woman who loved the truly specialness of both occasions, and because her beloved parents and family were no longer together, it was too painful or difficult to celebrate, as nothing else could compare.

    She saved all of her childhood art pieces, and even some of my Dad's. She had her mother's vintage fur and special clothing from the 1930's to 1950's. Her collections were fascinating and numerous, and they were quickly being boxed, trashed, or sold while I tried not to hyper ventilate. I can't blame my step-mom. This was hoarding to her, and she hadn't been there during the creation of these special memories, nor could she relate to Ginger's artistic process. I took home too many things and added them to my own hoard. I saved as much as I possibly could, without my husband divorcing me. I brought home vinyl records, ceramic pots, buckets of family photos and greeting cards, a rocking chair and stool, mirrors, art, metal patio chairs from the 40's and 50's, and more art supplies than I can convey. I dispersed many things to family members, but so much still went the way of the yard sale or trash can.

    My Dad would work on one area – a desk or drawer, while I worked in a corner of her art room. Meanwhile, Teresa would clear out an entire room. My Dad and I would trip down memory lane, or I would hear him sobbing so I would stop and grieve with him. Everyone processes death differently. My process is slow, and with every item I touched, read, and experienced, it brought me closer to Ginger. I felt that I understood her more, and loved and missed her, mourning the fact that we weren't close.

They decided to cremate her, and went back and forth on burying her at her mother's grave, or taking her with them to Georgia, along with the cremated remains of at least six of her former pet dogs. She loved her animals like they were people and throughout her life had never been without at least one. My Dad's wife, also a devoted animal lover, thought it appropriate to bury her and her dogs together, once they returned to Georgia.

Because they had changed plans a few times, and because you need certain permits to travel by plane with human remains, they eventually packed Ginger, the dogs, and mementos into a beautiful antique oak desk. The desk would be loaded onto a truck and transported, along with other people's things, across the U.S. This troubled me. Knowing that she was put in a desk drawer and loaded like cargo, along with the twenty or so boxes Teresa had packed. It didn't feel like the right thing to me, but I wasn't about to question them on it. I know they were doing the best they knew how in this unexpected and difficult situation. I was not present for the arrival, loading, and departure of the moving truck. Instead, I heard about it from my Dad. One of the guys loading the truck was not very sensitive to their situation, so a few words were exchanged, but an understanding was eventually reached.

That was it. The house remained nearly empty, except for some items I still wanted to go through in the art room, and the furniture items that would be sold by the realtor at an Estate sale.

My Dad and Teresa boarded a plane to Georgia. I went back to my home that was now crowded with bits of Ginger's life and memories. Ginger was in a desk drawer on a truck, somewhere in the U.S.

Except that she wasn't.

When the truck arrived at my Dad's home, nearly two weeks later, everything was there, except for the desk, and its contents, including Ginger. My Dad was devastated, and Teresa was furious. The desk was worth about four thousand dollars, so they think it was stolen; the thieves not realizing it had human and canine occupants inside. They contacted the moving company, but got very little result, since they hadn't insured their load. Nearly a year later, there has still been no sign of the desk or Ginger.

    I like to think that this was Ginger's final curtain call. Her last hoorah. She did things her way, throughout her life, so why would things be any different in death? Many didn't understand her choices and ways, but that was Ginger. She was an artist through and through. Eccentric, dramatic, difficult, with a biting sense of humor, and a deeply caring and thoughtful side. Details mattered to her. Heck, her life and her entire home were filled with interesting details!

    So, here's what I think. If spirits can affect what happens in this reality, I believe she had a hand in this calamity. I like to think that we didn't really lose Ginger, but instead she found her own way home. Just her and the dogs, maybe along a dusty highway, or near some artist's community. Maybe they were set free in a gentle breeze. Maybe they're still sitting in the desk, in some old hippy woman's house, along the coastline of Big Sur, listening to Cat Stevens, and being "Miles from Nowhere", just the way she wanted to be.

Gabrielle Symmes

# Finding Ginger

In every brush stroke
  And shadow of leaf
    And blue sky
I find you.

In the swallowtail butterfly
  Lighting delicately
    On the vibrant magenta bougainvillea flowers
In the wilds of your back yard
  I find you.

In the hoards of
  Photographs, sketches, greeting cards,
    Vinyl records, sea glass, marbles, jars of rocks,
      And random quotes,
        I find you.

In Jerome, Arizona
  Perched on a hilltop
    Overlooking the Verde Valley
      I find you.

In art
  I find you.
In beauty
  I find you.
In humor
  I find you.

In the spice rack
   And garden aisle
   In cookies
And soda
    In fairy tale
And in memory
   I find you.
Dear, Ginger.

   Not lost.
     Instead, I find
You are with me everywhere
   And always.

Gudelia Vaden

# First Day of School

Sobbing silently in my new blue checkered dress, I held my older sister, Socorro's, hand as tightly as she hurried me down the noisy corridor of Planada Elementary School in the San Joaquin Valley. In the late 1940's, and at four years and nine months of age, I was about to enter first grade. My older brothers and sister taught me numbers, most of the alphabet, and English.

Socorro left me at the first grade room, and hurried to fourth grade. I felt scared and missed the warmth of my sister's hand. I missed my mother. I imagined her soft and soothing voice, "mija, be brave." I wish my mother could have brought me to school, but she had to take care of a new baby and a toddler. I thought of better things to do than go to school, such as playing with my younger sister, Elisa, and pushing her in the stroller.

I was assigned to a brown wooden desk in front of the room because my last name began with the letter "D" for De Landa. Most of the students in the class were Hispanic and a few were Caucasian. I do not remember my teacher's name, but she rarely smiled. She wore horn rimmed glasses and was about thirty years old. My older brother, Paul, had warned me not to speak Spanish. If I spoke Spanish, I could be slapped or hit on the hand with a ruler. I tried as hard as I could to not speak Spanish, but one time I forgot and got a swat on the hand. I cried and I could not believe I was being punished for speaking Spanish. We spoke it at home.

I wanted to play, but there did not seem to be enough time for that. It was all work. I went home and asked my parents to talk to the school so that they could transfer me to kindergarten. My parents met with the principal, but he decided not to move me.

I had to adapt to what seemed to be a long school year. I liked recess, but it was short for a girl that liked to jump rope, swing, and play dodge ball. I had made a few friends, but they preferred to speak Spanish.

The best part of school was coming home for lunch with Socorro. We smelt the aroma of mom's flour tortillas cooking on the hot grill. I enjoyed putting butter on tortillas, which melted in my mouth. She also made pinto beans with cheese, chicken soup or enchiladas.

Looking back to that time in my life, I learned that a person should not be threatened for speaking in their native tongue. Students should have a supportive learning environment in which their self-esteem and culture is valued.

Gudelia Vaden

# Pieces

Pieces of things
Shreds of words
Wind-swept in the memory
Shrouded by years gone by
Clouded by storms
And gnarled, bare trees
Of Riverside in winter
With its chill
And new found rain
On bare land and orange trees
With a fragrant carpet of orange blossoms
As dead leaves lie, wind-swept
In a corner of a memory
As days go by

Gudelia Vaden

# The Season of the Empty Nest

On a warm Saturday afternoon in Riverside, a breeze was steadily blowing through the ficus trees. As I strolled in my garden, I noticed the empty bird nests. What was once a commune of birds was gone. I was reminded of a motel that flashes a vacancy sign. There is a time to build a nest, and a time to leave the nest. My children are grown, and have left their childhood home.

I have mixed emotions. On one hand, I wish they were all back home. I miss their constant laughter, and our son, Patrick, playing his guitar, sometimes through the night. I miss just being with them. On the other hand, I am glad. My daughter is married and my son is in a relationship. They have their own homes and careers. Our son Patrick is quite a chef. My favorite dish is crab legs with buttered wine sauce.

In 1986, our oldest child Natalie attended her senior prom. She wore a gown made of blue chiffon with short ruffled sleeves and a matching blue sash tied around her tiny waist. She resembled Cinderella. She waltzed around the house while she waited for her prom date. She was so excited, she jumped up and down. With stars and twinkles in her big brown eyes she asks me, "Mom, how do I look?" "Beautiful!"

I remember going on nature hikes in Yosemite National Park with my children. I can still smell the dampness of the leaves, the aroma of pine trees and the display of colorful birds of yellow, green and light brown. The beach was their favorite, especially the tide pools. Just lying on the sand filled my day with nostalgic memories. We told ghost stories at dusk when the moon was full.

When my children left, I thought parenting was finished,

but it goes on. We are blessed to have one granddaughter. The season of the empty nest will go on, as there is a time for everything under the heavens.

Thomas J. Vaden

# A Blessing in Disguise

    I dumped my motorcycle on my right foot trapping and scraping my ankle against the unforgiving curb. The damaged ankle swelled to ten times normal! Although not broken, the ankle stayed swollen for two months. One would think this is tragic, but actually I had a blessing in disguise.
    Disneyland is crowded and the lines are horrendous, but guess what! If you have an obvious handicap, you and your family go to the front of the line through a maze of side entrances. My children were happy to propel me in a wheelchair past the throngs of miserable bystanders. And, at the special shows, we were allowed in early and given special seating.
    Wow, we went on a dozen rides that day when normally we would be lucky to go on four or five. Thank God for the swollen ankle.

Thomas J. Vaden

# Sixth Grade

YOU'RE STUPID MISTER VADEN!

I had transferred from one school to another in the middle of sixth grade. I don't remember what I did to deserve that brutal insult, but, I do remember thinking I am not stupid, and I am going to prove my teacher wrong. After all, she didn't know me.

I have a vivid memory of the time she got angry and came running down the aisle, her rosary beads whirling in the air. These were not ordinary rosary beads, but were attached to the side of her habit, each wooden bead a half inch in diameter. If she had hit me with the beads, they definitely would have left an impression on my mind, as well as on my skin. However, half way down the aisle, her beads caught on a student chair, broke, and the pieces bounced all over the floor. This stopped her in her tracks, perhaps less than a few feet away. She shouted, "you're just lucky, Mr. Vaden, you're just lucky!" I felt that God surely must have been with me that day.

Towards the end of the school year, we took tests on what we learned. I passed these tests with flying colors and I graduated number two in my class, beat out by a girl! I was given public recognition by the nun, in front of the entire class!

Thomas Vaden

# The Old Shoe

I Don't Know
What I would do
If I were the woman
In the old shoe
My mom didn't know
What she would do
She was the woman
In the old shoe
She had five
When I was ten
My dad left her
On her own to fend
No money
No husband
No help
I grew up fast
I had to last
Today I'm grateful
For my past
My grandmother helped
She was a marm
To five kids revolving
In a bee like swarm
Today we are respectful
For our past
And not regretful
We are successful

Thomas J. Vaden

# Thoughts on Death

Some die young and some die old. My brother, Patrick, died having just turned 18 while in Okinawa in the Marine Corp. He died doing what he wanted to do. My mother had to sign permission papers, as he was only 16 years old when he entered service.

How can someone so young know what he wanted to do in life? What is the purpose of life? What must one accomplish before we meet our higher being? Do we have to accomplish anything? Death is rather permanent – I know of no-one who has come back to life, that is, life as we know it. Death is like our universe. We do not know what lies beyond the boundaries.

Where is my brother now – does his spirit survive beyond my memory? Will my memory and perceptions survive beyond death? How does one define survival? Only our maker knows.

Alan VanTassel

# Breakfast

My dad always woke me early. Even before he came in to roust me out of the sack, I could hear him in the kitchen, rustling around with frying pans, searching for ingredients in the refrigerator. First he would fry bacon and potatoes from last night's dinner. We always made a few more potatoes for dinner than we would need to have some leftover for breakfast. Dad would take the cold boiled potatoes out of the fridge, cut them up and fry them in Crisco. Last he would fry the eggs, two at a time, over easy. Runny eggs were the the only eggs on the menu. When he reached a point in the preparation of our breakfast, he would come down the hallway to my room and say, "It's almost ready, Alan. Time to put you feet on the floor" I would find out later in my life that the expression, "Feet on the floor" is a military expression. It is barked at recruits many times over in boot camp. Dad was just repurposing the phrase for me.

All the while, he would be listening to the local radio station, getting the local news and the weather. When the weather would come on, he would look out the window in the kitchen by the table and scoff, "I think I could have come up with that forecast, just looking out the window." Soon he would have his morning cigarette, Lucky Strikes, no filter. He would serve me first as I sat at the table, waiting. I wouldn't say much at that time. Soon the newspaper would hit the driveway. I would go out and get it, opening it up to read the headlines on the way back to the kitchen. I would start to read the paper. He would look over my shoulder, reading from a distance what I was reading.

Soon Dad would go down to Susan's door and start singing to her, "Wake up, little Susie, wake up!" My sister would drag herself to the table, then she would get her portion of over easy eggs, bacon, and fried potatoes. Orange juice was also on the menu. It was fresh squeezed in our home. My mother would take care of that chore the night before. She wanted to leave it time to chill in the fridge over night. My mother would soon follow my sister down the hallway to get up. Soon we were all reading our parts of the newspaper, the Chicago Tribune. One of my parts was the funnies. I would follow Peanuts, especially. I would laugh at the comic strip more than not. Then I would read it to everyone else and explain the drawings as I read it. Soon we would all have a laugh, if not about the comic, about the way I narrated it. Some in the group were not excited about hearing another narration of Peanuts. I would have to promise that this one was really funny. That pledge made me even more persistent about getting a laugh for some part of the narration. It was a tough audience, but I was rarely completely booed off the stage. Sometimes I would get crumpled paper napkins thrown at me, indicating my audience's' displeasure at my sense of humor.

My attention then would turn to the feature stories in the A section of the paper. My Dad had already had a chance to read it over. He had formed an opinion. I would quickly read over the beginning of the articles on the front page. I would offer an opinion, "Nixon will never make it! We all know better than to vote for him again, don't we." My mother would shake her head. Another argument was coming for sure. Dad would just roll his eyes and take another drag on his Lucky Strike before he took a sip of his coffee. He would do something with the newspaper I was never really ever able to duplicate. He would take out the crease in the middle of the paper (I have heard some refer to it as the "fold") by moving it just right, shaking it, making a sharp paper sound like no other. I was sure that I had hit a nerve. Of course it wasn't a surprise to me that it hit a nerve. I knew I had stepped on thin ice. Discussions about politics were never really resolved. When he thought the discussion was over, he would say, "Well, at least we got up before breakfast." Then there was silence around the table. Discussion over until the evening meal, when we would take off at the same point again.

This was the point in our day where we talked about the coming day, discussed where we needed to go and when, what time we needed to be home. This time was one of affirmation before we encountered the challenges of the day.

Years later, I was visiting my father and his wife, Betty, in their home. Dad was physically a mere shadow of himself. He had joked the night before that he didn't know why he kept seeing his father in the mirror. I have heard people say of those who had been ill for a long time. "He was just skin and bones." That would have been an apt description of the man I saw across the table from me. He looked tired even though we had just gotten up out of bed. Betty was making us bacon and eggs over easy, runny. He looked at me and said, "At least you got up before breakfast today." I smiled, appreciating the echo of our earlier days. It was very sad for me to then listen to him repeat that phrase three times as if he had not said it before. I finished my breakfast, talking about things that I was involved in, our little man, Keith, my teaching position, the play I was directing. Soon I left to return to my new life with my family.

On the way home I was listening to the radio discuss Reagan's meeting with Gorbachov in Iceland. When I arrived home about two hours later, my wife was in tears. She told me to sit down, then shared the news that Dad laid down on the couch when I left. Betty went out to get the mail and when she came back, she tried to wake him to give him his mail. She couldn't wake him. He was gone.

My wife and I returned with our son. We started to make arrangements and call the family to notify them. It just always makes me happy that my Dad and I got to have one more breakfast together and he remembered, "We got up before breakfast!", before he went on to his reward.

Alan VanTassel

# Those Summer Nights

When I was growing up we lived in a neighborhood of small post-WWII housing. If you measured the homes and the yards against the places we live in today, you would usually find smaller homes, bigger lots, and more people living in each home.

When my Dad was in the Army in the Pacific in WWII, my mother worked at the GE plant in the town where she grew up, Dekalb, IL. She was Rosie, the riveter. During the war, as my parents would say it, all the production activity was put toward supplies for the war. There were very few things to buy. Mom and Dad were married in 1942. He was already a Second Lieutenant. Mom saved most of their money while Dad was in the Pacific. She lived with her mother and hey pooled their resources to pay the bills. I have looked at the census materials on Ancestry.com and found the entry for my mother and her mother living together in DeKalb in 1940. They stated their income. I was measured in the one hundreds, not the thousands.

When Dad came home, Mom had already purchased a home in DeKalb for them to live in on South Second Street. My parents were married for a number of years before I was born. In that time my maternal grandmother, Anna Metcalfe, came to live with us. It was a natural outcome of my mother's affection for her mother. There were four other siblings in town, but they all had children and challenges of their own.

When I came along in 1950, the house my mother bought

at the end of the war was getting small. Dad was working for an engineering company. He and his crew were laying out a subdivision north of town. The Kishwaukee River flowed by the streets of Tilton Park. There were old stands of oak trees, sloping hills, and green everywhere. Dad found a lot that he really liked. It was a street and a half from the river, just high enough to avoid high waters. It was on the large side of a curve so that the back of the lot was wider than the front. Dad and Mom were the one of the first to buy a lot in Tilton Park. The street name was Delcy Drive. I don't know if they ever appreciated the alliteration of Delcy Drive in DeKalb. There was a builder in the subdivision building tract homes. Dad chose to contract the house himself while working full time. By this time, my mother worked in a law office. The lawyer helped my parents get set up to contract the home themselves. Dad set up a VA loan and began the construction of the house. Most of the homes in that area were what we called slab homes without basements. It was an added expense to put in a basement. Dad thought it was worth it.

There were many advantages having big family in town. One of my uncles was an electrician. He wired the house for us. Another uncle was a home heating contractor. He supplied the furnace and the other uncle installed the furnace for us. Dad did much of the framing, the insulation, the flooring, the painting, the siding and so on. This house had hardwood floors in the bedrooms, plaster walls and tiling in the bathroom. The first painting of our house was grey with red trim. We had a detached one-car garage and a concrete driveway that sloped slightly down from the street. Dad would get my mother to gasp every time we drove in the driveway. He would turn in and put the car neutral and his foot off the break. He would let the car roll into the garage and hit the back wall with a thud. Soon the back wall of the garage bowed out from this little game my Dad played. It was his garage. He could do with it as he pleased.

Springtime was planting season. We planted a garden in the back yard every year. We would plant a couple of rows of sweet corn, even though we never got many ears from the corn stalks we planted. We planted tomatoes, green and yellow beans, peppers. In mid to late summer, we would have a pile of each to share with family and neighbors. Each year we would plant trees and bushes around the yard. There were no old stand trees in our yard, but just behind us was a couple of lots there were just full of old oak trees. My Dad put in a white plank fence along the back lot line. It extended over three lots to the back of us. Dad made a good pick of lots.

Springtime and summer brought weather with it as well as planting. Most weeks brought with them rain storms complete with lightning and thunder, the kind of lightning and thunder that really shakes you at the core of your soul. The weather always came from the Northwest. Since our house faced the West we could sit in our front room and watch the storm coming. Sometimes we would sit on the front step and watch the sky go darker and the thunder and lightning get closer. We could see the lightning on the western horizon as it approached. We could hear the thunder from afar. I learned that if I counted the seconds between the lightning and thunder, again and again, I could accurately predict the direction and the proximity of the storm. When I heard thunder, I would look for the lightning and begin to count. If the two got closer in time, then I knew the storm was getting closer. Another indicator of the proximity of the storm was a change in temperature. Usually in that time of year, the air temp would feel warm. When a storm was approaching, I would feel a whooosh breeze of cold. Sometimes there would be hail, some small and some large, snowballs falling from the sky. Then came the warm. At this stage in the storm we all knew that it would be good to take cover. There could be a tornado coming. We would listen to the local radio station to find out if there were any predictions. Tornadoes are fickle storms. They come from nowhere and disappear as quickly. After a tornado, there would be some streets completely destroyed and across the street homes would be untouched. There was much oral history about tornadoes. Older people would tell about the shelter they had in the barnyard. It always made me think of the "Wizard of Oz". I wondered out loud if I would land in Oz if there was a tornado coming through.

Alas, there was always more preparation for a tornado than the real thing. Since our house was one of the only in the neighborhood with a basement and one that didn't fill up with water when there was a storm, the neighbors would come over to take shelter in our basement when we thought there was enough of a warning to take shelter. Naturally, we would try to make these times more of a community gathering time, but there were enough of our neighbors who knew more about tornadoes than they ever wanted to know. Some would pray. Others would talk about their experiences with tornadoes. Many would try to change the subject. Many times during these storms I could hear the rain beat against the siding on the house. I could hear the water splash in waves sometimes against the little basement windows. Since those windows were not made for these storms, the water would come in. This turn of events would make some gasp and pray harder. At the height of the storm, the noise of the storm would drown out our voices. Silence was called for. The worst though was always inevitable. The electricity would go out and there would be darkness in the cellar. The void of light would panic some and kids would cry and pray they would live. We could hear the wind breaking branches and the branches crashing against the house. Periodically there would be hail. The sound of hail falling on a house is distinct. It's the sound of a thousand baseballs hitting the side of the house, the windows and the roof at the same time. When the wind turns and the storm bounces off a picture window, it can be frightening. From the basement we could hear all of these sounds. A homeowner is thankful for a good roof when all of this stormy activity is taking place.

I was always thankful that storm like this didn't last forever. When we know the storm had passed we would poke our heads out to assess the damage. First we would look to see if the house was still on its foundation. It was not unusual for a tornado to lift a house off its foundation and the inhabitants below in the cellar would not know until they came out that the house was gone. We would assess the tree limbs to be removed from the yard, trees still standing and the roof to see if all the shingles were in place. It was not uncommon to find our shingles in the neighbor's' yard or vica-versa.

What I loved about the end of a rain storm was the smell of clean. The rain seemed to wash away all the filth in the street for a time. It smelled humid and clean, akin to the smell of getting out of the shower. Storms are a part of our lives, because without the storms how could we have the sunshine? The aftermath of a storm is a cool summer breeze in my life.

The thing that lasted about the end of a storm was the feeling all of us who had huddled in the cellar had for the other. We shared a moment of time where we didn't know if we would survive. It was scary and we had pulled through. Some of us didn't know the other very well, but this moment in time pulled us all closer together. Days after the storm neighbors would bring cakes or cookies by as a thank you for sharing our cellar. When we saw each other in the neighborhood, we would talk about our families and the members' progress in life. In the evenings that followed, we would gather with our neighbors on our back porch for Bar-B-Q.

When the weather was balmy and cool our summer evenings were spent on the the screened porch on the back of our house. Neighbors, family and friends would come by to visit. Dad would share his beer or a glass or whiskey. Mom would share the latest thing she baked, cookies usually, chocolate chip. I loved them. The best part of those evenings was when I would sneak up behind my Dad's chair and steal a drag on his Lucky Strike or a swig of his Schlitz beer. Those nights in our neighborhood were so quiet. Some would say with a chuckle, "It's so quiet I could hear the corn growing". We kids would chase the fireflies in the back yard. Each of us would have a Mason jar with one of those sealing caps to slap on it when we managed to get a firefly in the jar. We would have a contest to see who could get the most in each of our jars. We would all put grass cut from the yard in the jar to make the firefly feel better.

As it got darker, the fireflies would sparkle yellow on and off rhythmically. When there was more than one in the jar the spark of the light coming on was more staccato. Our jars would serve as lanterns in the dark. We were sure each time that the flies would be there alive for us in the morning. It was disappointing to go out to the porch and find the flies dead again even though I did my best to punch holes in the cap for air. Soon I learned that it was best to let them go at the end of our evening. They would be out there for me to capture again on another summer night.

Dale Vassantachart

## A Day at Joshua Tree National Park

Early morning is the best time of day
Before the fierce summer sun's rays
What will we see
At Joshua Tree?
"49 Palms Oasis" marks one of the trails
With barrel cacti red spiked nails
Low shrubs are parched and tan
In the canyon spring California palm fan
Sitting in the shade of the oasis
A spiny tail lizard creeping beside us
No sightings yet of a Joshua tree
So we hike back as fast as can be


It is mid-morning, temperatures are high
We want to see more as time flies by
What will we see
At Joshua Tree?
We view monstrous boulders of granite
And Joshua trees from another planet
Their arms are seen in the air
Like the Prophet Joshua in prayer
We hike the trail to Barker Dam
Scanning for bighorn sheep, ewe and ram
Along the overhang of the cliffs
Looking up at Indian petroglyphs

It is half past noon, to the Visitor Center we go
To show the Park Ranger what we know
What will we be
At Joshua tree?
The Junior Ranger badge is to be earned
Answering park questions of what we learned
Our Junior Ranger booklets are nearly complete
In the museum, we finish the feat
The Ranger greets us and reviews what we did
Asks us questions and says, "good job kids"
The pledge, the badge, we are proud to be
The Junior Rangers of Joshua Tree

Romaine Washington

# Helium

she jangle gold
leaf feet
her head cartwheel
tailbone of glitter
a tiara tumbling in
black taffeta
twirl two times
on tiptoe
 ball bounce tall
snatch steel stars
from sidewalk galaxy
where gravity
does not exist
sh-sh-sh-sh-sugar
shake it away
rainstick
drip
yellow
chalk
hummingbirds
swirl round her
startled hair
in raucous laughter
like hail
falling skyward

Romaine Washington

# When Palms Breathe

wind shutters
the back
      of her neck
                s h e  g l i d e s
into
wakefullaughter
eagles dream her face a rockycrag
         s h e    e a r t h s    b l u e
leaves       paint skin
and mud
legs dance treelimbed wisp
hand      into
pebbled     prayers
     stop
a fawn  to gaze
s  p  i  n  s    herself into a  r  i  b  b  o  n
arms s  p  a   n the rootsofeyes
     pray is a song
that swallows
     clouds and sun

Romaine Washington

# Ground Swell

her life a wild weed
growing in stubborn
sidewalk cracks
earthquake fault line
cracks
side    walk into
mornings
dust-brown air
pushing up against
blue dreams
at St. Anthony's    on 16th
nun she plans to be
none black like she
walks to
New Hope
Mission    airy    Baptist
Church
walks on Sunday
eats chocolate manna voices
      *We are soldiers in the army*
      *We got to fight – oh yes we got to fight*
books her weapons
library basic training
not sure who's the enemy
sometimes herself

mama at work to clothe and feed
brother somewhere
he ain't supposed to be

latch key she
walks to
SB High
on E Street
Carousel Mall - E Street
first home of Golden Arches
E Street
        no E Ticket
        blood red bird
        concrete crimson
        casket classmates
        devoured by cracks
most times she play
soft ball - skateboard - bicycle
over cracks -
keep movin'
study how to fly
cardinal
flap and dip
community
SBVC
#61 in Cali
CSUSB
in front of classroom she
feeds hope to
new latch key

she say
we are not

                a massacre
                a most murderous statistic
                a homeless den of         hopelessness
we are not      a nameless label of numbers

we are home
sifted by the Santa Ana's
brown
pushing up
against blue dreams

San Bernardino

# Tesoros de Cuentos

Frances J. Vasquez

# Tesoros de Cuentos

During a spirited Unity Poetry event on the Main Street Pedestrian Mall in Downtown Riverside, Juan Felipe Herrera, then-California State Poet Laureate, encouraged an enthused crowd to, "Value our parents' and grandparents' stories... Value your own stories, and most of all, your voices... celebrate your voice when you make enchiladas and tamales. Celebrate your beautiful voices. Share your voices."

I was inspired to help write down the beautiful voices of the Mexican American community - their unique experience. A litany of ideas ruminated in my imagination, as I visualized an opportunity to elicit the wealth of bicultural stories held in the hearts and memories of "our gente" through custom writing workshops. So, I recruited Rose Y. Monge, the best bilingual and bicultural memoir teacher in the region to help facilitate a memoir workshop. Thankfully, she accepted. Together, Rose and I developed detailed lesson plans and launched our cuentos writing group in the Barrio de Casa Blanca. Our goal was to help the participants discover their beautiful literary voices.

Rose and I launched the Tesoros de Cuentos workshops during 2016 National Hispanic Heritage Month. We conducted six-weekly workshops at the SSGT. Salvador J. Lara Casa Blanca Library, located in the heart of Riverside's oldest, predominantly Latino neighborhood. The following summer, we reconvened the cuentos group for six more workshops that culminated in the submission of their wonderful, well-crafted stories to the Inlandia anthology.

We designed the workshops in a bilingual, bicultural format to help participants flesh out and write the fantastic cuentos waiting to be released from inside their hearts. We hoped they would write those hidden treasures: stories perhaps unknown to younger generations; cuentos that may have been passed on from one generation to another. In a friendly and supportive environment, participants wrote down their stories, their memoirs from their own perspective.

We encouraged participants to chronicle what life was like back in the day. We aspired to help them give voice to their unique stories about family, school, and their community. A treasure trove of sweet and savory recollections unraveled as we reflected on abuelitas' favorite dichos: those wise sayings that taught us life lessons. We incorporated food in our cuentos journey. Food is a basic ingredient of life; and, stories about it yielded reflections of larger life lessons. We revisited childhood memories of Mama's incomprable tortillas; gatherings at abuelita's house to make Christmas tamales... and the annual family Thanksgiving feasts.

It took the village of Casa Blanca to give literary voice to the stories that were created as a result of our cuentos workshops. Thanks and appreciation to the Casa Blanca Community Action Group for allowing me time on their meeting agenda to discuss the proposed workshops, and solicit their help. Gracias del corazón to Roberto Murillo, Bob Garcia, and Morris Mendoza for their wisdom and support. Thank you to the staff at SSGT. Salvador J. Lara Casa Blanca Library and Catholic Charities of Casa Blanca for providing a comfortable, welcoming place for us to meet and write. Heartfelt thanks and gratitude to Maestra Rose Y. Monge (and kindred Sonorense) for her generosity and support. Special thanks to the Inlandia Institute for a successful partnership, and for publishing our cuentos. Most of all, mil gracias to the amazing cuentistas who shored up the courage to express their beautiful literary voices for the first time. These emerging writers gave us much to appreciate: their creativity, diligence, and wealth of stories (many more still waiting to be written). *Aplausos* to: Maria Jaquez, Morris Mendoza, Angela Maria Naso, David Rios, and Scharlett Stowers Vai.

Frances J. Vasquez

# Tesoros Dorados ~ Golden Treasures

*My daughter | my necklace of precious stones | you are my blood | you are my color | you are my image | ... you are noble | you are precious | you are turquoise | you have been shaped by the gods...*
~ Nahuatl Praise-Poem

The scions of Eliza Tibbets' two imported Bahia Navel orange trees reigned supreme in Riverside. The prolific mother trees became the genesis of a thriving citrus industry - the golden tesoros that made the region prosperous. Through grit and ambition, local, out-of-state, and foreign investors transformed Riverside's arid landscape into miles of lucrative citrus groves. It wasn't always this way in Riverside and its environs.

What might the region look like before European/Anglo migration? By expanding one's imagination we can visualize the early inhabitants of the Inland Valleys, who for millennia were nomadic, hunter-gather peoples. Local indigenous people lived in small villages subsisting on the abundance of plants, fruits, nuts, seeds, and the wild life native to the region. Ostensibly, native peoples migrated with the seasons to other regions to hunt and gather food. Much like migrant agricultural workers do today, they "followed the crops." Steve Lech writes in "Pioneers of Riverside County," that Spanish explorers Pedro Fages and Capitán Juan Bautista de Anza came here from Sonora, Mexico to establish an overland passage. Their scribes kept detailed notes about their encounters in the 1770s. The landscape of the region was primarily a Sonoran Desert-like environment. Nopales and other cacti, agaves, and other California native, draught tolerant plants, brush and trees were abundant.

The Bahia orange trees flourished in the region's fertile

sandy loam and sunny "Mediterranean" climate. Irrigation from the Gage canals gave the groves the water of life they needed to thrive. Aided by favorable railroad routes and the readily available cheap agricultural labor facilitated a land boom in the region during the 1880s. Tom Patterson wrote in "A Colony For California," that in 1885, Riverside was named the richest city per capita in the U.S. With visions of wealth from the orange gold, people migrated to the region to seek their fortune and a better lifestyle.

The arduous, low-wage jobs the citrus industry offered were filled primarily by the strong hands and backs of people of color. First Asian, then mostly Mexican workers labored in the citrus groves and packing houses. Immigrants from México came here primarily to work, and enhanced socio-economic opportunities for their families. In the late 19th century, Mexican workers began to settle in Riverside's Casa Blanca neighborhood, centered on Madison Street in the South-central part of the City.

How did Casa Blanca get its name? Joan H. Hall wrote that in December 1878, Louise LeGrande Lockwood and her son, Henry Benedict Lockwood, migrated from New York to live in Riverside for health reasons, and moved into their large new two-story, white-plastered adobe home on Magnolia Avenue near Madison Street. They called it Casa Blanca, for "white house." The Lockwoods planted 60 acres in citrus trees and a small olive grove. The property and the general area promptly became known as Casa Blanca. Soon, Mexicanos, when describing the area to others, would express, "Allá, por la casa blanca…"

The brutal 1910 revolution in México caused a wave of mass migration of Mexicanos to the region. Like many emigrants in Casa Blanca, my paternal grandparents came from Michoacán to escape the ravages of war. The large influx from México during the revolution resulted in a welcome labor pool of cheap labor in Riverside (and throughout the Inland region). The workers were an economic boon to the citrus industry that thrived on keeping labor costs low and profits high. Unlike other immigrants who ventured solo to the United States to seek their fortunes, Mexicanos traditionally have brought their families along with them.

The developers were strategic in creating the Casa Blanca neighborhood. In February 1889, Samuel Cary Evans Jr. filed a subdivision which he called "Map of the Village of Casa Blanca." It originally consisted of almost 20 acres, divided into 74 lots. By creating the Casa Blanca subdivision, Evans Jr. "achieved two objectives. From a personal business standpoint, he created a source of income from town lot sales. And, from an economic and social standpoint, he provided a logical place where workers could own homes close to the products that needed picking and processing." To be sure, the location was strategic and sensible, as it was located in the midst of thriving citrus groves. Also, the proximity to the newly established Casa Blanca train station made logistical and economic sense.

Irving G. Hendrick posits in "The Development of a School Integration Plan in Riverside, California: A History and Perspective" that numerous labor camps and settlements had been established along the Santa Fe railroad tracks to support the burgeoning citrus industry. Several were established in Casa Blanca and its environs, and in nearby Arlington.

The Casa Blanca subdivision provided affordable housing for families, and an alternative to the labor camps. Bill Wilkman, in his article, "Casa Blanca's Evans Street" describes a once-bustling Evans Street corridor with numerous packing houses and small businesses. Because the street ran parallel to the railroad tracks, it was advantageous to the citrus industry, and to the workers. The developers also wanted to ensure that the trains that traversed the area would not impede the workers' accessibility to the citrus groves and the packing houses. Waiting for the trains to pass was not an option.

But, the residents did not have a school for their

children in Casa Blanca, nor much else in infrastructure and amenities. Young children who were fortunate enough to attend school had to walk one mile to the nearest school. Most of the older youth were unable to stay in school, as they were needed to work to help support their families. These youth usually worked in the orange groves as "ratas" picking up the fruit that had dropped to the ground.

While education was important, it was nearly inaccessible to the children of Casa Blanca. Like most parents, Casa Blancans wished their children to be literate and educated. So, they began to hold meetings to develop an effective plan of action to best convince officials to build a school in their Barrio. They decided to circulate a petition and gather as many signatures as possible to present to the Board of Education. Because most of their employers were powerful civic leaders, the activists had to use discretion to protect their jobs. We can imagine them meeting in the patios of their back yards, in the privacy of their humble homes, perhaps quietly, in the evenings and on Sundays. Circulate the petition, they did.... Like México's "las Adelitas" of Revolutionary War fame, a pair of brave mothers volunteered to present the petition to school officials. One hot July evening in 1911, two Casa Blanca women attended a meeting of the Board of Education of the Riverside City School District. They went for one purpose only: to present a petition officially requesting that the District establish a school in their neighborhood. Representing the Casa Blanca community, they addressed an all-white, mostly male school board; the lone woman was Stella Atwood, a feminist and civic leader, who would become Casa Blanca's champion on the Board of Education to establish a school for their children.

According to the minutes of the July 11, 1911 school board meeting: "A petition was presented signed by eighty residents of Casa Blanca, asking for the erection of a public school in that locality. It appears that more than seventy children of school age reside in Casa Blanca: those forty children in primary grades now go to Victoria School."

Lamentably, the women's names were not noted in the Board minutes, and they were not identified in the newspaper report the next day (like they did of Anglo males). They and the eighty signatories on the petition served as Casa Blanca's cultural bearers in pursuit of access to education for their children. Sadly, their names, their true identities have been lost to history. Why they were not named is a mystery, but probably a sign of the times. Nevertheless, the nameless duo is akin to México's folk heroes, "las Adelitas".

Finally, a school...! Hendrick documented that a school was established in 1913 for kindergarten and first grade in makeshift classrooms in an abandoned warehouse on Prenda Street. The school served the "predominantly Mexican American community in the area." In about 1918, the old wooden structure was moved from Prenda to Madison Street in the heart of Casa Blanca (more or less where the SSGT. Salvador J. Lara Casa Blanca Library is presently located).

In July 1923, the Board of Education elected Mabra B. Madden as principal of Casa Blanca School. Unfortunately, that school building also burned. The school district commissioned noted Riverside architect G. Stanley Wilson to design a new school that would be constructed of poured, reinforced concrete, a method of construction that was fairly new at the time. Meanwhile, the new highly-motivated principal went throughout the neighborhood to introduce himself to the parents, and worked hard to organize informal classes with the students in the community. The new Casa Blanca School was erected in 1923 at 3020 Madison Street, and proved to be a highly durable method of construction, as the old school structure still stands today.

During Madden's 41-year tenure as principal, he understood and acted upon the merits of racial and ethnic diversity of his school faculty. He hired several teachers of color, including Leo Baca, who Madden appointed as Vice

Principal, and Gloria Elizarraraz, a former student and resident of Casa Blanca. He hired a young Hazel Russell who would become the District's first African-American teacher. Despite Mrs. Russell's previous attempts to land a teaching position in Riverside, no one would hire her. Madden followed his keen instincts and established a precedent by hiring Russell in 1947. Dr. Russell became a distinguished school administrator and college professor.

In 1965, the District appointed Ernest Z. Robles, the first Latino Principal at Casa Blanca. He was a former student and became a prominent educator of national renown. Robles was tasked to implement the District-imposed shuttering of Casa Blanca Elementary School. Robles served in significant administrator capacities, and later founded the National Hispanic Scholarship Fund based in Northern California.

Despite strident protests and petitions by Casa Blanca parents and the pillars of the community, the School Board voted in March 1967 to close Casa Blanca as a regular school to implement the District's controversial, yet eventually acclaimed desegregation program. The District closed the school in June 1967 and in September, Casa Blanca students were transferred by bus to other schools within the District. The plan continues today - to the dismay of Casa Blanca parents and community leaders.

The school site was repurposed and the State of California operated a Pre-school for local children. In April 1977, the School District held an auction and sold the Casa Blanca School property on the south side of Madison Street to the Catholic Diocese, who was the sole bidder. Currently, the old school buildings are vibrant with activity by the ministries of St. Anthony of Padua Catholic Church, and with Catholic Charities, which established an outreach office at the school annex to serve the local community.

The "village" exists today as a distinct Riverside neighborhood. The community of Casa Blanca remains predominantly Latino, and most of the residents dearly value their family-oriented, tightly-knit community. As they should.

I respectfully pay tribute to the pioneer activists who spawned a cadre of future community leaders. The two mothers and the petition signatories made sacrifices, shored up their courage, and took a bold public stand for the sake of their children's education. And, they most likely accomplished this with limited English-speaking skills. They are the *tesoros* on whose golden shoulders have supported the many future leaders; the pillars of the community who have emerged in Casa Blanca. The enduring legacy of "Las Adelitas" and their activism has left an indelible mark in the history of education equity in Casa Blanca, and Riverside. This is the stuff that makes for good books... and movies.

Nobel Laureate William Faulkner, in his iconic 1949 prize acceptance speech, extolled the inexhaustible voice of man, capable of compassion, sacrifice, and endurance; "the writers duty is to write about these things... by reminding him of the courage and honor and hope and pride and compassion and pity and sacrifice which have been the glory of his past... the pillars to help him endure and prevail." Faulkner's ideas are as relevant today as last mid-century. Indeed, it took courage, honor, hope, pride, compassion, pity, and sacrifice for "las Adelitas" to lead the school effort in Casa Blanca - and we rejoice. To them, I offer an ancient Nahuatl poem of praise: "Aqui estas mi hijita, mi collar de piedras finas, mi plumaje de quetzal, mi hechura humana...". Thank you, necklaces of turquoise and gold. you are noble | you are precious | you are turquoise | you have been shaped by the gods...

Where are we now on the school issue? Members of the Casa Blanca Community Action Group have worked continuously with Riverside City officials for almost 50 years to develop, plan, and implement infrastructure, capital improvements, and other benefits to the community. To their credit, the Casa Blanca CAG has outlived the other CAGS formed by the City in other parts of Riverside in the late 1960s.

It's apparent that the indomitable spirit of "las Adelitas" flourishes in the DNA of Casa Blanca community activists and leaders. Currently, the CAG has made it a priority to work with school district officials to establish a new elementary school in Casa Blanca. Impressed and inspired by Tesoros de Casa Blanca exhibitions of vintage photo images of the beloved old school (and class pictures) from the collection of Roberto Murillo, the area school board Trustee expressed his commitment to revisit the issue of neighborhood schools. Enlightened by new education pedagogies and analyses of the District's past practices, officials are now considering strategies to build a new school in Casa Blanca. They recognize the educational and social benefits to the students, and the implications to the entire community.

Expect book and movie deals when the new school in Casa Blanca is established. The ghosts of "las Adelitas" and the pillars of Casa Blanca will jump for joy. For they will not merely endure, they shall prevail.

*I wish to thank and acknowledgement Roberto Murillo for enlightening me of the two Casa Blanca women who petitioned the Riverside school board, and for his love of Casa Blanca. Thank you, Jo Scott-Coe for encouraging me to write this story.*

Frances J. Vasquez

# Parable of the Rings

**Prologue**

Virtuosa was a wise and generous woman. She devoted her life to serving God and humanity. Virtuosa dedicated herself to an illustrious career of helping people have a better understanding of other cultures. She taught people to value and appreciate ethnic diversity. Virtuosa was a sophisticated world-traveler who was keen to the ways of people. She was born and raised in Altahuerta, and lived and worked in metropolises like San Francisco and Mexico City. She purchased property in Villa del Sol, a retirement community in Southern California, where she planned to settle in her future golden years. Virtuosa reasoned that she would only be a short drive away from her two older sisters who lived in Altahuerta. Virtuosa normally made time to be home at Villa del Sol for the Christmas holidays. She was blessed with many old friends and plenty of family members with whom to share the glorious Christmas Holidays.

**Season of Giving**

One Christmas, Virtuosa treated her elderly sisters in Altahuerta to a feast of roast turkey, yams, vegetables, fruits, boxes of assorted See's chocolates, and other delicacies. On Christmas Day, her many family members called to greet her, as did her dear friends: June, Gallagher, and Lacey. Two of her late brother's daughters heard that Tía Virtuosa was in town. Since it had been almost a year since they last saw her, they wished to visit their kindly aunt. The nieces phoned their Tía and made plans for a visit on Christmas evening.

Virtuosa's nieces, Candida and Alegra drove together from Rio Seco to see their beloved aunt. Tía Virtuosa made them feel welcome and offered them food and drink. Candida presented her Tía with a small gift. As Virtuosa opened it, a bright smile illuminated her serene face.

"It's an appointment book to help organize your busy travel schedule in the New Year," said Candida, the elder of the two sisters. "Oh, honey, how nice of you to think of me," replied Tía Virtuosa in her sweet, loving way.

Tía Virtuosa, a smart, worldly woman had acquired a bit of wealth, and appeared to have everything she could ever want. So, Candida selected a practical, modest gift for her Tía. Alegra had not bothered to take a gift.

After a while, Virtuosa excused herself and retreated to her bedroom for a few minutes. Upon her return, the two younger women respectfully stood up. Tía Virtuosa extended her arm between her two nieces. In the open palm of one hand she held two rings: a lovely golden ring featuring a faceted Peridot gem stone. The other ring was a simple, Tigers Eye stone glued onto an expandable metal band, seemingly by a hobbyist.

Candida deferred to her younger sister with a nod of her head, indicating to Alegra for her to choose first. Alegra chose the more valuable of the two rings. Then, Candida picked up the remaining humble ring. Both nieces thanked their Tía Virtuosa for her generous Christmas gifts.

While the three women were still standing, Tía Virtuosa, without saying a word, removed a Diamond cluster ring from her own finger and handed it to Candida. It was a surprise! Tía's precious ring was adorned with several small Diamonds encircling a larger one in the middle - like a brilliant daisy set on a white gold band.

**Moral**

Virtuosa, through her unspoken deeds, modeled the virtues of giving and generosity. She demonstrated that it is better to give than to receive.

Maria Jaquez

# Hace Diez Años

It's been 10 years.
Our relationship was always stormy and prickly.
Sometimes I thought you hated me.
Sometimes I thought I hated you.
You could be so mean and hurtful.
And, I admit, I was no angel.
But, you were my mother, and I loved you.
I never understood why you were always comparing yourself to me.
You didn't get to go to school like me, and you were always afraid I would leave you behind.
You watched too many silly *telenovelas* about ungrateful kids.
But, I was your daughter.
I never felt better than you. I just wanted you to be proud of me.
We were different in so many ways.
You loved driving. I have always hated it.
I loved cooking and baking. You hated those chores, even on holidays. You used to say a holiday for you was a day you didn't have to cook.
You were good with your hands. I was better with books.
You did beautiful crochet work. I still have your lacy doilies, the purple tablecloth.
When I decided to learn a craft, I chose knitting.
You had a green thumb. I don't. I've murdered every unfortunate one that has crossed my path.
When I was growing up, you didn't even like cats. I love cats.
I am the consummate cat lady.

But, we also had a lot in common.
We both had a sweet tooth. Nothing is too sweet for us. Not like abuelita Golla who often found deserts *"empalagozos."*
We were like abuelito Jose.
We both loved fruit and vegetables. We both liked nopales. They say they are good for regulating blood sugar levels.
We both loved roses.
I taught you to love cats, and you taught me to appreciate telenovelas.
And you taught me about fairness and justice.
When I came home from grade school one day and I told you my teacher had said that many of the slave owners were good people and cared about their slaves, you called her a "vieja loca".
Hace diez años que te fuiste. Pero, se que estas bien. Estoy segura que el Roro te acompaña.
El Roro was your beloved, ornery cat who lived to be 20.
And, I'm sure you are feeding him *chicharrones* every day.

Morris Mendoza

# The Viet-Nam Era and My Block Friends

I remember the Viet-Nam era between 1965 to 1972, and my "block" friends. These memories are about Gerald Zamora, Bernardo, nicknamed "Third" Renteria, and "Baby" Louie Rocha.

Other neighborhood friends also served during the Viet-Nam War. When I say neighborhood friends, I think of guys who I went to school with at Casa Blanca Elementary and Chemawa Jr. High. Some went to Sierra Jr. High and then on to Ramona High School. We also spent time in Boy Scouts; riding our bikes and other things. We did fun things from childhood to our teenage years.

None of us ever joined a gang. At one time we had the idea of starting a club called the Smokers. But it never came to be. I think it was because most of the guys were individuals, not followers, not wanting a leader. Or, maybe because their parents would not approve.

Well, going back to the Viet-Nam era. Most, if not all, of my neighborhood friends were graduating from high school. Also, during that time our nation had something called the Draft. So, some of my friends decided to join the military service rather than be drafted. No student deferments for us.

Some of my friends did not go to Nam. Randy Paramo spent his time in Alaska. My cousin Albert Mendoza did stateside duty and Richard Rivera went to Germany. And, I went to South Korea.

But most of the guys from CB that were drafted or joined, ended up in South Viet-Nam. Two of them ended up dying there: both Henry Pasillas and Henry Gomez. To be clear, there were many other Riversiders who did their duty and also paid the ultimate price by being killed or wounded during the war in South Viet-Nam.

So, my best friend, Gerald Zamora volunteered. He became a crew chief in a helicopter unit. I think his helicopter got hit once and crash-landed. I believe his only injury was losing some teeth. He used to man a machine gun in the 'copter. He would always volunteer to go out and support the ground troops.

My second neighborhood friend I like to mention is Baby Louie Rocha. Some names had the word "Baby" attached to them as a way of meaning "Jr." Well, I believe the war took the biggest toll on him. He died before any of us. I feel he had PTSD before it was diagnosed.

The last friend I want to mention is "Third" Renteria. Third served in our Engineering Unit driving heavy equipment. He was no fool. When asked, or ordered, one time by his Lieutenant to go out to scout for his unit, he was ready to do so. But another soldier volunteered to take his place. The soldier never came back.

Well, my friends all came home and married neighborhood girls. Two are still married to this day to the same women. Bernardo Renteria and Gerald Zamora used their G.I. Bill to get their college education. Bernardo and Gerald are now retired and are volunteering at our local V.F.W. Post 184 and Team 40, an honor guard unit based at the Riverside National Cemetery. Bernardo worked in Human Resources as an investigator in Workmen's Comp. Gerald worked in many jobs, like a railroad mechanic and for the Western Municipal Water District.

I am so proud of my Block Friends. They are true American heroes in their own right.

Morris Mendoza

# Memories of Madison Street

Madison Street, named after the fourth President is probably the most important street to me in the city of Riverside. Most important, because it was the street I used the most to get to where I wanted to go in my community of Casa Blanca. I used it to go to my schools; to go to my church; to get to the Lomita. My friends and I built a tree house on a Walnut tree on Madison, before getting to Victoria Ave. I use Victoria Ave. today to get my walking exercise. I also am currently a member of a Riverside group called Victoria Forever. The group, when possible, plants donated trees and keeps the Avenue clean.

My Grandfather had a grocery store on Madison named Mendoza Market. It was a mom-and-pop store which he owned for 50 years. Attached to the store were a post office and a barber shop, which he also owned. I worked as a stock boy at the market, and I sometimes helped customers at the cash register. I liked helping my Grandfather but I did not like working there.

Today, our neighborhood library is named the SST. Salvador J. Lara Casa Blanca branch. It's named after a hometown Medal of Honor recipient. I am proud that when people drive down Madison Street, they can see his name on the library.

Morris Mendoza

# Relationships Through the Years

My first childhood friends were my cousins who were close to my age on both sides of the family. On my Dad's side, there were my cousins Albert and Rudy, my Uncle "Chapo" Milton's sons. Albert was my age and Rudy was two years younger, like my brother Charles. When we were five years old, we lived in two separate homes but on the same property my Grandfather Victorio owned.

My Uncle Tony had two daughters, Martha and Veronica. I had more cousins, of course but they were either older or younger than me.

On my Mom's side of the family, I remember mostly playing or being with my cousin Vangie, who lived with our Grandparents and her mother, Angie. I remember riding horses with her on my Uncle Baltazar's small ranch on Colorado Street which was about three miles away from Casa Blanca Street. Other times I would go visit my Grandparents, who lived on Railroad Street. Vangie loved parakeets and so did I. She gave me a blue parakeet once, called Beauty. A short time later, Beauty flew the coop. My cousin Lillian was Vangie's younger sister. Lillian was my age and I still have a few pictures of us together at my Uncle's ranch.

When I started school, I counted most of my classmates as friends. There were a couple though, that I was scared of because they seemed to be tough guys. Some of my best friends in elementary school were Ralph Lopez, Richard Rivera, and Randy Paramo. I don't know why, but I guess it was because we got along together.

I remember going to Randy's house and playing in his back yard. One time, during our middle school years, I used to lift weights with Richard. We were in a fitness fad after seeing movies with actors like Steve Reeves. My other friends were my street friends. We used to like to walk to the Lomita which was a couple of blocks from my house on Santa Rosa Way. I found out later that the Lomita was really named Quarry Hill. On the back side of the Lomita was what we called the "canyon." But it was only a very big hole where granite was quarried. My friends would climb up and down the little hill, going down into the canyon. When it rained, the canyon filled with water and formed a pond. There were a lot of tad poles in the pond and we tried to catch them. Other things we did together was to build a tree house on a Walnut tree on Madison Street not far from my house on Santa Rosa Way. We also built little forts and tunnels on an alfalfa field on Victoria Avenue.

One other experience I had with my neighborhood friends was joining the Boys Scouts. Boy Scout Troop-19 had about 40 Scouts. We were divided into about four different (groups) that we called Patrols. My friends and I who were small in size decided to call ourselves "the Peanut Patrol."

I believe sharing these adventures formed a bond with my street friends that I still have with some of them today.

In elementary school, I had my first girlfriend when we were both about seven years old. We were both teased by some of our fellow students. At junior high, I had a crush on a girl who was from a Southern state. Maybe it was because of the way she spoke with a Southern accent. Anyways, I made her laugh one time by sticking a pencil between my upper lip and mouth.

Morris Mendoza

# Tortillas and Me

I really don't have many childhood thoughts of food, but there are a few memories. Before my Dad passed away, he would make us a simple treat of tortillas cut in pieces with butter. He liked his chile, and his favorite was Chile Negro, also rolled up in a tortilla.

I have to say that my Mom's tortillas were the best. That's one of the two best foods she made. Of course, they were hard to make. I still think I can smell them cooking on the comal. The masa, the lard, the white flour, and her rolling the dough and sprinkling the flour.

The other favorite dish she made was what I called "scrambale." It was a red chile sauce meat dish and vegetables, mostly potatoes. These are the two dishes that I miss the most. Although my Mom taught my Wife to cook, my Wife turned out to be a better cook than my Mom. My Mom's scrambale is still the best. Rosie does not make tortillas at all, but she makes tasty menudo and good caldo.

Again, the tortilla was the most important food for me growing up since I did not use silverware until I was in junior high. The only time I cooked was when I was in the Boys Scouts to earn a merit badge, or when we went camping; we ate mostly things out of a can like baked beans, Campbell's chicken noodle soup, and corn. So when my two Sons were in grade school, we formed a Cub and Boy Scout Troop with the help of St. Anthony's Church and the Home of Neighborly Service. It lasted about four years.

When my uncle Balto had his small farm, I think of the time they killed a steer and had fresh meat. It was the first time I saw an animal being killed. I was about eight years old.

It was a gory sight, but the meat tasted so good after it was prepared. I still can remember the man who was in charge. His name was Santiago.

When I was in the service, I got the first taste of Army food. We would be forced to rush to the chow line, and eat our food so fast... not much flavor in that. I got stationed for several months at Fort Sill, Oklahoma. The Mess Hall was a big cafeteria where you got to pick your food. Boy! What a difference!

One time on off-duty, I visited the town of Lawton by bus. On that trip, I walked to the edge of Downtown and found a little Mexican restaurant. It felt so good eating Mexican food with tortillas after a month of just eating Army food.

There were a couple of other eating experiences that I like to think about. One was eating a pizza made by an Army buddy, George Sutton, who worked part-time at a pizza parlor off-base. We ate pizza with a dark beer, listening to a table juke box. Never had a better pizza experience!

The other eating experience was not a good one. The national dish of Korea is kimchi, a cabbage that is fermented and really smells bad. But, the Koreans enjoyed it. I did enjoy a dish called something like "yaki mandu," a bowl of rice and potatoes - simple but tasty.

Well, to conclude, I'm thinking of the tortilla again, mostly the flour kind, not the corn ones this side of the border. It may sound crazy but when I attend Mass, I think of the altar as a table where the dead and the living come together to eat, and the Host reminds me of a small flour tortilla!

Rose Y. Monge

# Train Trip with my Nana

    I might have been four or going on five years old when Nana tells me she has a surprise for me. Would you like to go with me to Nogales, m'ija? I turn my gaze towards Mami and she smiles shaking her head up and down. I've never been outside Agua Prieta and never on a train ride. Nana is an accomplished seamstress who sells embroidered linens and kitchen towels to tourists and occasionally travels by train to her destinations. Mami, why is she going and not me, my sister cries out. I'm the oldest! *Callate por favor,* Trini. You've taken many trips with your Nana. Now it's Yoli's turn.

    As the day approaches, Trini taunts and annoys me daily pulling my braids, hitting or shoving me "by accident" and glaring at me. She's never been to Nogales and I feel a bit sorry for her but not for long. Just because she's the oldest doesn't mean she can get her way by whining. Where and how far is Nogales from Agua Prieta? I don't know and I don't care and I'm giddy for days.

    My heart is pounding when the big day arrives. As I dress, my sister gives me the evil eye and pinches my arm for good measure. I want to punch her back but she's bigger than me so I only stick out my tongue at her—leaving her sulking. Nothing is going to ruin this day for me. Walking into the kitchen, I notice two burlap bags resting on the floor. With Mami's help, Nana picks up the larger one and straps it onto her back. She's a tiny lady not much taller than me. How is she going to carry such a huge bag? Mom gives me the other smaller one and I sling it over my shoulder.

    We speak in hushed voices so not to wake the others up. Trini continues pleading and lamenting to no avail. Mami hugs, kisses me on the forehead and cautions me to be a good girl as she hands me a small paper bag that smells like papas and chorizo. Hand-in-hand with Nana, I step into the morning darkness. Am I really going to be inside a train today? I give my Nana's hand an extra squeeze to thank her. She smiles warmly and tells me to watch my step on the uneven and unpaved road. The blurry lights of the train station, a good distance away, beckons us forward.

The more I walk, my shoulder begins to hurt and now the bag full of linens feels like bricks pulling me sideways making me lose my balance. I try switching it to my other shoulder but it doesn't help. Nana reassures me that we're almost there. *Pacienca, m'ija.* Rays of sunlight begin to peek through the darkness as we slowly make our way. At last, we arrive at the Agua Prieta train station in Sonora, Mexico. Another world enfolds before me teeming with people of all ages, shapes and sizes moving to and fro. A short, dark-skinned woman with a baby straddled on her hip balances a basket on top of her head with one arm. Two toddlers cling to her rumpled apron. She looks too young to have three babies! A weather-beaten, old vaquero tips his sombrero in our direction and smiles broadly unconscious of his missing teeth.

People carrying chickens and roosters who are clucking in wire cages add to the ruckus. Look, Yoli. There's a bench, Nana points out. I'm breathless as I sit down! Nana is also out of breath as she sits down for a few moments but tells me she needs to go inside the train depot to get our train tickets.

Before leaving, she advises me not to talk to anyone or let anyone take the bags. I don't know how long she's gone and nobody bothers me but I keep the bags close to me just in case. *Tienes hambre, m'ijita,* Nana asks me when she returns. *Si, mucho hambre,* I respond. She opens the thermos bottle and removes the cap and pours hot chocolate inside it and hands it to me. Ah! Mexican chocolate! Chocolaty and cinnamon-y!

Gracias, Nana. I retrieve a burrito from the paper bag. Do we have to sit here for a long time? No, not long...*pacienca, m'ija*. Nana always says *paciencia* when she wants us to be quiet. I turn to my burrito and devour it in a few bites. I slurp my chocolate slowly and quietly not wanting to upset Nana. I dangle my legs back and forth and begin counting the throng of people passing in front of me. I count and count and then lose count and start all over again. I get to 50 when I notice that it's much quieter now and everyone's attention is directed to the left side of the train depot and towards the railroad tracks in the distance.

And then I hear a faint rumbling... becoming louder, louder....until it's thunderous.....with each passing second. Clickety clack, clickety clack. Click-a-de clack. Click-a-de clack. Chugga-chugga-whoo-whoo. The station trembles and soon billowing waves of soot and steam are stinging my eyes. I almost fall off the bench when the squealing brakes from the iron dragon breathes its final gasp and jerks to a sudden stop.

As if on cue, the crowd darts as if one body towards the boarding steps. Grab your bag and find us a seat, m'ija, Nana shouts out. *Apurate*, Yoli ... and don't worry. I'll find you, *te prometo*. I rush forward dragging the bag on the ground as I follow the herd of passengers to the open doors. The steps are too high and I stumble a few times. Where's my Nana? I need her strong reassuring hand. Once boarded, I see an open space and run as fast as my little chubby legs can carry me. An old splintery wooden bench will do just fine as I wait for Nana.

As the passengers lay claim to seats, the ruckus escalates becoming unbearable fueled by the clucking of the chickens and the roosters. The wire cages placed on the floor are preventing the harried passengers to move forward. Some people just jump over the cages grumbling and shaking their fists at the owners. To get a better view, I stand on top of the bench praying not to fall. Still clinging to their mother's apron, the two toddlers are wailing uncontrollably now. Poor momma!

The older vaquero with the toothless smile approaches me and lays two leather saddles near the bench. Hola, niña! My throat is dry but I'm awestruck that he can speak without teeth. Not knowing what to do or say, I blurt out, have you seen my Nana? No, he replies. Sit down, niña, you're going to get hurt. I want my Nana, I whisper. Still standing, my eyes dart back and forth. My body is aching and I have soot in my nostrils. I dwell on my discomfort in silence but glad the vaquero is nearby. I know he's talking for I see his lips moving but don't hear a word he says. Then, he tugs my arm. Look, chiquita…is that your Nana over there? He waves his two arms in her direction. I breathe a sigh of relief as I see her making her way towards me. (This would be the first and only trip I made with Nana.)

David Rios

# Living in the Shadow of the Panama Canal

My excursions out of the borders of the U. S. A. have put me in situations to experience how it feels to be in a "foreign" land and to be a minority, a stranger in a strange land, the "gringo" in "Latinoland."

My family of origin consists of Mom; Dad; brother, Tony; I am number two in birth order; followed by sisters, Missy and Mamita.

My life has been governed by Dad's philosophy that someone with a Spanish surname should be able to speak Spanish. (I don't know that I can clearly state why. Perhaps there is some orgullo / pride involved.) It has taken me decades to more fully understand and embrace that philosophy for myself, but I did not require it of my children.

My second trip to Panamá as a child covered a five-month period—the longest, continuous stay in all the trips taken to that country over the years. While all the family, parents and the four children, went down together, Dad returned stateside to continue with his job after a short period of time.

Travel on Pan American Airlines was vastly different from what airline travel is today. The meal, included in the price of the ticket, was eaten with metal utensils (not plastic). Towards the end of the flight the stewardesses came around with warmed 100% cotton wash cloths to help one freshen up before landing. These and other "courtesies" have long since disappeared.

The heat with humidity that greeted one at the Tocumen International Airport was a jolt. Passengers had to walk outside the airplane, down the steps maneuvered in place by the ground crew, and on to the tarmac before heading into the building, like we had to do at the Ontario Airport in the 1970s and 1980s when there were no "jetways" to keep one in air conditioned comfort.

My Tía / Aunt and Abuelito / Grandfather each owned one side of a duplex in the corregimiento (subdivision of a district) of Betania. They lived in one side and rented out the other when we weren't there for an extended period. Each unit had two large windows in front and two on the back side with a screen and two wooden shutters that closed over the screen and were secured with an eye & hook (not very secure in my young opinion). There were no bars on the windows as is often seen in Panamá. Along all the exterior walls, the top row of cinder block had holes in it, which were covered by a screen for protection against mosquitos and other insects. There was a front door and a back door directly opposite each other that had a screen door and a wooden door with a regular lock. There was no central nor window air conditioning units, so it could get hot during the day—however, it would cool down during the night.

In the interior, two walls formed a "T" with the shorter segment forming the living room-dining room area. The longer segment was a divider between two bedrooms. In keeping with the idea of taking as much advantage as possible of any sea breezes, all the walls of this "T" did not go clear to the ceiling. Therefore, conversations were not really private. Sound carried and reverberated from the painted concrete floor to the zinc roof. (We children did know how to "raise the roof" with our chatter and other noise.) All this was important to four children ranging in ages from 3 to 11. On at least one occasion, we took advantage of this architectural feature to start in one bedroom; climb over the wall into the second bedroom; go out the door (a curtain on a curtain rod); run through the living room-dining room; in through the door (curtain) of the first bedroom to repeat the process. We were aided by the fact that there were beds against that common bedroom wall in both bedrooms. We kept it up for a while, probably working in "camper" pairs. (We had been paired off so the first and last born were one camper pair and the two middle children were the second camper pair.)

To complete the description of the house, on the common wall of the duplex, there was a bathroom occupying the front portion, and directly behind that, an alcove off the dining room that served as the kitchen with a two-burner stove and a stainless steel sink-drain board combination.

I don't recall a television on this visit. Even if there was one, unless there was an English station available (and there might have been one, living so close to the Panama Canal Zone), we didn't watch it. I do recall Tía reading the newspaper, at least on Sundays. In Tía's bedroom she had a record player with a few records. The only one that I remember was a male vocalist singing: "One, two, three o'clock, four o'clock rock…, We're gonna rock around the clock tonight…" This may or may not have been Bill Haley and the Comets. Looking this up on the web, the words are slightly different than I remember, but then, since I sometimes change the words to suit my fancy, it may have been he.

There was a radio that was on at times. (Even if it was not on, one could hear the music or commentary from one or more neighborhood radio(s). The only advertisement jingle that I remember from that time was "¡No diga café, diga café Durán! (Don't simply say "coffee," say Durán [brand] coffee!)

In the neighborhood, on the opposite side of the street in front of the duplex were several "row" houses with common walls. Behind the house, there was a similar row. However, starting on the side of the duplex that fronted the busier street, after our duplex the houses were individual ones with no common walls. The busier road had a steep grade. The buses (the size of small school buses seen locally today in Southern California) coming down the hill downshifted, the ones going up the hill pushed on the gas pedal—there was a lot of horn honking and other noise coming from that street. Across that street was a school. Every Monday morning traffic was stopped while the national anthem (Alcanzamos por fin la victoria… / We finally attained victory…) was sung by students and teachers while the red, white, and blue Panamanian flag was raised. In the evenings on the quieter street in front of the duplex, the neighborhood children would join in games similar to what we played in Maryland.

From first grade through my Bachelor of Arts Degree, I attended private schools run by the Seventh-day Adventist Church. My stint in Panamá was no different. However, the twist here was that Tía was the principal of the school as well as the second grade teacher, my teacher. We usually sang a hymn as part of opening exercises. Since I didn't know the words in Spanish, I have been told I made my own up (which probably made no sense…). Out the screened windows (with no glass), one could hear the noise of the street traffic and see an apartment building that was several stories taller than the school (and served as distractions as needed). To keep me occupied on my own personalized school plan, Tía kept me busy making up mathematics problems (which helped me learn to love and appreciate math, until I hit fifth grade back in the U. S. At that time we went to the "new" math, which I learned to hate). She gave me Spanish workbooks which I still have to this day.

That school, of which I cannot recall any specific name with the instruction in Spanish, was actually held in the (Caribbean) English-speaking church. The Spanish-speaking church we attended on Saturdays was in another part of the city. It was next door to a printing press business. If I wanted to zone out from all the Spanish being spoken, the noise of the press was an easy distraction and my thoughts could take me anywhere except in the real, present moment. The wall around the sides and back of the church was similar to others in the neighborhood—six – seven feet. As the top of the wall was completed, a liberal amount of cement was placed there and then jagged pieces of broken glass of different shapes and colors were inserted into the cement (to discourage people from climbing over it). From our Sabbath School room, on an upper floor, one could look down on a section of the wall, which was new to me. In Maryland I was used to three-foot chain link fences, if there was a fence at all, separating one property from another.

Tía had a small car, which she used to transport students before and after school. A memorable occasion for me was a graduation ceremony that Tía, another teacher colleague, Tony, and I attended. It was a novel experience held in a very large, brightly lit auditorium. However, more excitement awaited us after the ceremony. Upon returning to the car to leave, we found that someone had stolen the back two tires. Logically, cars carry one spare tire, but how does one resolve replacing two tires at one time? There were no cell phones in those days. While I could worry at the drop of a hat, this situation was beyond me. There was nothing for me to do but stand around. How Tía resolved the situation was unknown to me, but we did finally make it home some time later on four tires. It even appeared in the newspaper with a picture of the car in its reduced state.

For many in Panamá, car ownership was not an option—it is a small country and cars were expensive. However, the bus system was quite extensive. Besides the buses already mentioned, there was a type of bus called a chiva / goat. These were smaller, had room for maybe eight people or so; presumably ran on fixed routes, but one could ask for a stop just about anywhere. Perhaps chiva was an appropriate name, since it tended to butt in and out of traffic. Looking back, this was probably an introduction to driving methods that didn't seem quite as concerning, but more like life as usual in my later, larger city experiences in Buenos Aires, Argentina; Montevideo, Uruguay; and Mexico City and Monterrey, Mexico.

There was a section of Panama City near the waterfront that included "Las Bóvedas," an original part of the City's defense against pirate attacks. I was attracted to it and could imagine Henry Morgan or other pirates attacking and those within the wall defending their homes and families. A short distance from this defensive wall, I was put off by a large open air market. To my northern sense of smell, this was overload to the highest degree—pungent, unfamiliar aromas. Years later, the open air market in Monterrey, Mexico brought these younger memories to the surface! A similar smell can be had in Los Angeles even today which is vastly different from our traditional grocery chain smell experience to which I am usually accustomed!

Food plays an important part in everyone's life. It was no exception for me in Panamá. There was the "comfort," familiar food like rice and beans. Both Mom and Tía made a sofrito / base of oil, garlic, onions, celery, cilantro, and tomatoes. This was best done in a paila / round bottomed, cured, cast iron cooking pot. Once it was ready, the sofrito was added to the black or red beans that had been cooked separately. It certainly added to an enhanced taste compared with beans without this addition.

Plátano frito / fried plantain were allowed to ripen (maybe more accurate to state almost over ripen), and when fried, they were VERY sweet! This is different from the use of plantains when they are green, which the Puertorriqueños call tostones and Panamanians and others call patacones. Another culinary delight was fried yuca /cassava root or a more complex dish called carimañolas in which the yuca was boiled, put through a grinder, and made into an outer shell within which meat (or vegemeat in our case) constituted the inside. It was then fried to a golden brown–delicious!

Another fond food was pan micha. These were small, individual servings of white, light, fluffy bread that had a soft crust and I could pull the softer inside out and insert other things like queso fresco / fresh cheese or mantequilla maní / peanut butter. However, if left out for the rest of the day, without putting them in a sealed environment (plastic bag or other container), they became rock hard!

There were many businesses that did not change their name when they went south of the U. S. border. Tastee Freeze was one such entity. Tía would rotate and take one of the four of us children on an outing from time to time into downtown Panamá City that would involve a stop for ice cream as part of the excursion. These were special moments because, as the only sibling present, each did not have to compete for the adult's attention and, once again, it was a SWEET treat and a reminder of Dairy Queen in Maryland and Virginia.

Closer to home was a grocery "chain" called Riba-Smith (pronounced "Reeba-Smeet"). It did a bustling business since it was located on a main thoroughfare, La Transísmica / the Transisthmian Highway. My being about 8 years old and my brother, 11, we would not be allowed to go to Riba-Smith by ourselves. However, with Abuelito along with us (maybe it was the other way around), we would walk the back way, over a creek and a well-worn path to get to the store. We didn't buy too much on any single occasion because what we bought, we had to carry back home.

There are many varieties of palm trees with different uses. I have come to appreciate hearts of palm used in some Mexican dishes. However, what I have not seen again since my childhood are the palm trees that produce pivá fruit. While it is not sweet (one of my main criteria of taste when I was younger), once it was cooked and ready to eat, it did have a pleasant enough taste.

Other different, but sweet, foods that I liked were Dulce de quayaba / guava or membrillo / quince and served with "queso 360" a fresh cheese eaten almost daily that had a pleasant, salty taste. Another was "Chicha de avena con canela." Chicha referred to just about any drink (fermented or unfermented). Our version was unfermented with milk, leftover oatmeal, cinnamon, and sugar put through a blender. (We didn't get that every day or even regularly.) In season there were some grape-size fruit that came several to a stem that had a harder green shell and a soft interior with liquid that one sucked off the seed. In Panamá these are called mamones, but in other parts of Latin America they are called quenepas. The inside that I remembered was white, but in other varieties the inside was more orange. The taste was sweet, but was eaten in an undershirt since the juice stained what it touched.

Ripe coconuts were a special treat. The children would watch as an adult, usually Abuelito or Tía, would crack it open with a machete. The hard meat was then grated and used to make arroz con coco / rice with coconut. If there were left over pieces not needed for cooking, we children would each get some. One would think that a coconut is a coconut. However in my book, all coconuts are NOT created equal. When the coconut is green and fresh and one can hear liquid inside, most paysanos / fellow countrymen would relish a cold drink of "pipa" as well as savor the soft meat once the nut has been opened. However, because of the different smell (or because it is not as sweet as the mature coconut, I had to hold my breath while trying to chug all the liquid, or at least as much as possible in one breath, and then shudder when I took a breath and had to deal with that awful (my perspective) taste! Yuck! Worse was when I was offered the "delicacy" of the soft meat. It was slimy and not fit for human consumption. Nowadays I can take a deep breath in anticipation and slightly enjoy the cool coconut water on a hot day, but I am more than happy to defer my piece of the soft meat to someone who would appreciate it more than I ever could!

There were other definite dislikes in the vast array of tropical foods. Since Tía started her day early with student transportation, she would sometimes cook plantain cereal that I imagine came from the store like cream of wheat (possibly in a bag instead of a box). By the time we children got around to eating breakfast there was a disgusting film on the top. Underneath it the cereal was better, but a bit grainy, not smooth like cream of wheat, and the taste/smell was stronger than cream of wheat.

In a category by itself is nance fruit. Thinking I might

have had an unreasonable memory from childhood, I tried it again in the late 1970s in Mexico—my impression or regard for nance had not changed—the smell and taste were a resounding turnoff!

Not quite as bad as nance fruit, but not in my realm of sweet foods is tamarindo / tamarind. It may have the color of dark chocolate but it sure doesn't taste like it! This is another "delicacy" that I have continued to willingly allow the next person (like my wife) to fully enjoy!

I did enjoy the national holidays. It would probably have been the celebration of Independence Day on November 3. There were performers dressed up—the women in their "polleras"—very colorful, full length plus extra yardage to flap around, hair all dolled up with combs, beading, etc. The men wore "montunos"—white embroidered shirts with black pants with a distinctive hat performing traditional dances.

A slogan that I heard was "Sea Panameño y cuenta en Balboas." That somewhat bewildered my mind. There was no Balboa paper money. There were the coins to make up a Balboa (1, 5, 10, 25, and 50 centesimos which were the same size as U. S. coins), and even a one Balboa coin. The bills used were U. S. currency. So, to the "Sea Panameño y cuenta en Balboas" was added by some "pero page en dólares" / but pay in dollars.

If I ever got homesick for "the States," a short, quick trip would place me in the Panama Canal Zone. While it was still tropical, there was a clear distinction between building codes and green spaces between Panamá and the Canal Zone and I could imagine myself back in the States with more English being spoken, commissary foods with familiar brand names, etc. Some of the rides were with Tía taking a short cut to get to another part of Panama City. Other times I think Mom was driving a car borrowed from a family friend. We even went a time or two to the Miraflores Locks of the Canal. It was exciting if we hit the scenario just as the compartment with a ship was almost to the level of the next one and the lock doors would open and we could see the ship move into the next compartment. But if we had just missed that process, it took a long time (to an eight year old) to fill or empty the next compartment and my mind would wander.

While these experiences were eye-opening and added greatly to my understanding of a different way of being, I was very happy after those five months to return to Maryland and continue my life and schooling in more familiar surroundings!

As I return from memory lane, would I visit Panamá again? I haven't been back since 1980. Both Abuelito and Tía are no longer alive. There is an uncle, who lived and worked in Virginia for many years, who has returned to the country of his birth. He came up for a visit this year. So I would probably visit locations that I have not yet seen before returning once again to Panamá. However, if I were on the way to Machu Picchu in Peru or Bariloche in Argentina, yes, I would make a stop in Panamá.

Scharlett Stowers Vai

# Who am I?

Who am I?
I was raised Chicana, but I'm not Chicana.
Who am I?
My mother told me that I have American Indian (Choctaw Nation and possibly Cherokee), Irish, and Black blood. I am classified Black. I don't look Black.
Some say I look Cuban. Some say Puerto Rican, even Panamanian. Some think I'm Creole, thinking I am from Louisiana.
But, who am I?
I speak with a Mexican accent; I am bilingual. I speak, read and write Spanish fluently.
I have Mexican mannerisms and sayings. I cook Mexican food perfectly.
But, who am I?
In a world where one is expected to belong to one race, I don't fit into these limited categories.
My first attempt to enter UCR as a Black student, a Black official denied me entry. Guess I wasn't Black enough. But, after an interview in Spanish, the Chair of Chicano Studies said I was Chicana; he approved my admission to UCR as a Chicana student.
Who am I?
Many say I have the ways of Native Americans because I am so open and giving - with a heart not of this world - a "pure heart."
Who am I?
Some do not like who I am. They say I'm too open and honest. They make me miserable by trying to change me. Trying to

force me into those limited boxes that will never accommodate me. There is too much of me to fit into those limited boxes!

Lonely? I used to be lonely. In my own home I was lonely. But in my Casa Blanca Barrio, I was loved and valued for being me, no changes necessary.

I am Carlota, ChaCha, Scharlett, "La Loca", and to some, Carla. My cousins call me Charly, and Alvino called me Chucha.

Who am I?

All who love me call me by different names, due to cariño; a feeling one cannot describe in the English language because it is felt.

After many years, I was finally officially admitted into the Brown Berets, Chapter 46.

Who am I?

Feel me. That is the answer.

Scharlett Stowers Vai

# What Does Casa Blanca Mean to Me?

Casa Blanca is Home, Love and Acceptance. My place in the family and in the Barrio de Casa Blanca. Learning another language and customs.

It's where I was born and raised by an entire community, along with my birth family.

I have a rich background because I was raised in two cultures. I learned to speak both English and Spanish, and many customs.

I was taught self-discipline; how to behave in public with proper manners. I was taught to have pride in who I am, and where I come from.

I was encouraged to go to college by my brother Eddie, and the Granmas in the Casa Blanca neighborhood, who never finished elementary school: "Mama Lola," Dolores Martinez, and "Granma Nacha" Ignacia Gomez.

I was taught how to care for my home and family for when I would have a family of my own. I was taught compassion and acceptance of all peoples, even the Japanese who were once our enemy.

Casa Blanca, to me, is a big nurturing family. Growing up, everyone looked out for each other. When some of the neighbors went to Fresno to pick grapes (in those days no one locked their doors) the neighbors would take care of their homes, gardens, and pets until they returned.

We had our own post office; Sophie the clerk handed out our mail and sold stamps. We had family-owned stores where we could get credit for goods when needed. There were even gas pumps to fuel the cars in Casa Blanca. Mr. Yoshida had one on Peters Street, and so did the Reyes Bros. Market around the corner on Madison Street.

    The name of the street where my family lived has changed three times. When I was born, it was called Opal Street. Because there was another Opal Street in another part of the city, the City of Riverside changed it to Peters Street. Later, it was changed to Ysmael Villegas Street where I live today in my grandmother's house, next door to where I grew up.

    I am here to stay.

Scharlett Stowers Vai

# Bruno

I'll never forget that summer. In seventh grade at Matthew Gage Junior High School when I was 11 or 12 years old. Summer had already started - I always loved the summer time! It meant I was going to Tulare, to spend the summer with Aunt Emma and Uncle Dave, and cousins Isabelle and Dwayne. They were more like my other big sister and brother than my cousins. They were really good to me.

In Tulare, I was welcomed and free to be a kid, and I loved it! One summer, I didn't go to Tulare. I don't remember why. It turned out to be a summer I'll never forget. The most wonderful thing happened! I was introduced, by my friend Margaret Romero and her Dad Joe, to his nephew, they called Junior. His name was Bruno Romero, Jr. We hit it off right away! One look at me, he fell in love with me. His uncle was very pleased.

We talked, we laughed, and his uncle Joe took us cruising around my neighborhood, my beloved Casa Blanca. I felt on top of the world! Most of my life I was lonely. I had no kindred spirit. No boyfriend. I had lots of "boy friends," and that's just what they were "friends." We were always together, shooting marbles, sharing thoughts and feelings. They loved hanging out with me, and I with them. The few girlfriends I had were beginning to have boyfriends. I had none.

Why? People might wonder why. It was because I am a Negra. Everyone in my barrio is Mexican and I am not. There was a "silent," but strong taboo. No race mixing. I accepted that fact, but I felt it was unfair. I always knew that the heart knows no boundaries, no limits. It was free to feel, to love: whomever it chose. There were some "boyfriends" I felt that twinge of a possibility for, but inside my mind, I knew there wasn't a chance. So, I pushed the thought out of my mind. There was no hope. I knew my place and stayed there.

There were some guys who were interested, but my "boyfriends" told them to stay away from those feelings toward me, that I was their friend, almost like a sister, so I was "off limits!"

I was a sad teenager; I wasn't allowed the luxury of having a boyfriend, like all the other girls my age and in my group of friends. Sometimes, I was glad I didn't have a boyfriend, witnessing, first-hand, the pain those boyfriends caused. I cried inside with them, but never shed a tear.

I couldn't cry. I was not allowed to cry. My mother would not allow it. So, I always smiled, happy or sad, I smiled. One cousin-in-law even called me "Smiley." It was embarrassing, but, that was just how I was. Happy-go-lucky, that was me.

The next summer was different. I was looking forward to seeing Bruno Romero, Jr. We had met the previous summer. This time I was allowed to bring him home with me. To go swimming in our pool. My parents seemed to like him right away. Guess they thought he was another "boyfriend." Good for me, cause I was smitten with Bruno and he was smitten with me. He was really good looking. He had brown slightly curly hair, and a light complexion, like mine. He also had hazel eyes, like mine, but his stood out more than mine. His eyes were a bright green hazel color. He had a perfect build in that his physique was in good proportion. He was slightly taller than me. I was quite skinny, under 100 pounds, with not much of a figure, but a tiny waist, less than 24 inches.

Bruno liked everything about me, I was told by his uncle Joe and his cousin Margaret. That made me beam. I think I'm in love! We swam and talked about a million-and-one things, we even kissed a few times. I felt my soul come alive, I felt high! "Would my feet ever touch the ground again?!" I didn't care, Bruno was there with me. My little sister snuck a few photos, but I didn't care. Bruno was holding me in his arms and I was in heaven! He said he never though he would ever find someone like me.

I thought "but I'm no one special, I'm not even pretty." I had this blondish hair and fair skin. I was always teased by my family because of it. But to Bruno, I was Cinderella and he was my Prince Charming - here to rescue me from the pit of pain and loneliness. I wanted to make a family with him. I knew our kids would be beautiful. Well, summer was ending, school would be starting, and Bruno would be going back to San Diego. I had family in San Diego. It wasn't that far. But still, I wouldn't see Bruno again, till summer. This made me sad. The old pain and loneliness was coming back with a vengeance! "Could I die while I'm waiting for my Bruno to come back?" At times it felt like it!

Spring vacation came for Bruno a week earlier than mine. I received a phone call from his cousin Margaret that he was coming! Coming during spring break. I was elated! It was a long time till summer. Would he still love me? Had his feelings for me changed? I was both worried and excited. These feelings frightened me. Finally, the day was here. In a few hours Bruno's uncle Joe would pick me up. Oh! The anticipation was killing me! When I walked in the door at Uncle Joe's house, I was almost inside, when I saw Bruno. He rushed toward me and hugged me tighter than I had ever been hugged, even by my brother Eddie! Again, I felt that rush of happiness I always felt with Bruno.

High school changed everything. I lost contact with Bruno. I wrote him letters, but he never responded to my letters. The sadness came and went. I just accepted it, and concentrated on my goal to go to college. Eventually, we lost track of each other.

I found high school so boring that I couldn't wait to go to college, so I even went to summer school. My goal was to attend the University of California, Riverside. Despite my mother telling me that I wasn't smart enough, my brother

Eddie encouraged me. He said. "I know you can do this." He even supported me by taking some classes with me at UCR. In the first quarter at UCR, I earned straight "A's" for the first time in my life. Now I showed my mother and Mr. Coleman that I made it in spite of them. I felt on top of the world! I felt there were no boundaries as to where I could go from here. But, I met my husband-to-be and decided to get married. I quit school because my husband didn't want me to go. He wanted me home to raise kids. So, I quit and raised a daughter. When my baby was four months old, I divorced him due to the fact that I found out he was a heroin addict, and I saw that he would never change.

A few years ago, perhaps in the 1980s, when I was working at the Casa Blanca Pre-School, I ran into my friend Margaret, Bruno's cousin. I was her four-year old son, Paul Villegas' teacher. I asked about Bruno. She said he had gotten married and I think she said he had no kids. Then the sad news came. She said, "Junior died in a motorcycle accident and was burned alive." I couldn't believe it! Such a beautiful man, burned to death. My heart sank.

I made my re-entry to UCR, but had to quit due to financial reasons, and attended Riverside City College where I majored in Early Childhood Studies. I was offered a job to teach in my beloved Casa Blanca. I wanted to give back to the community that had given me so much. Because I was bilingual and a resident of Casa Blanca, Grace Bailon, the librarian at Casa Blanca Library recommended me for the vacant position of afternoon teacher at the Casa Blanca State Pre-school. I worked there for 11 years.

And, now I still can't help wondering how my life with Bruno could have been. "Maybe, in my next life we will find each other." Can't wait!

Scharlett Stowers Vai

# Alvino

Alvin Aparicio was my grandmother's next door neighbor and my good friend. I used to spend hours at Alvino's house. He treated me like gem. I was his little girl. He called me Chucha, a term of endearment. He said it meant Jessica, but my friends said it meant "chatterbox."

I did enjoy talking to him. He listened to me and taught me many things, especially Spanish words. Alvin was an avid reader; he was very intelligent. He spent time in the Army during the Korean War. He had trouble with his feet due to "jungle rot," A form of athlete's feet, a type of fungal infection that never went away. Alvin also had gout, a form of arthritis that caused his feet to swell, and wouldn't allow him to walk or go to work as a loader of Citrus fruit, especially oranges at the Blue Banner Packing House in Riverside. All the men in his family picked oranges. Because he was strong, he loaded the big boxes.

Alvin was an active alcoholic. My mother and grandmother took care of him when he would get drunk. My mother would take us kids to the local bar or cantina on Evans Street in Casa Blanca to pick up Alvino and bring him home to put him to bed. Sometimes, he would sneak back out, but my grandma was vigilant and would peek out her front door and catch him; showing him a "switch," and saying "Get back in that bed and go to sleep!" One time I especially remember Alvino came over our house so drunk he could hardly stay awake. He passed out in a kitchen chair and my mom used her hot curlers to curl Alvino's straight hair. Soon, he woke up and to his surprise, his straight hair was curly. He said, "I must have really gotten drunk, it curled my hair." LOL! It was too funny!

When my parents remodeled their kitchen, we ate at Alvino's house for a few months. Alvino was a good cook. He made homemade tortillas, but best of all, I loved his chile con carne. We even ate Nopales from our yards. My dad only liked them with eggs. I love Nopales with chorizo. My dad loved chorizo so much that we called him "The Chorizo Man." He even added chorizo to rice and hominy - separately, of course.

My mom worked four different jobs: The U.S. Post Office, California School for the Deaf, substitute teacher for Riverside Unified School District, and as a Commissioner for the Housing Authority. And, she served as a consultant to various agencies. She was gone a lot, but she always made sure we had all we needed and wanted. She even took us places: San Diego Zoo, Disneyland, and Mooney's Grove in Visalia, CA. I spent summers in Tulare, CA near Visalia.

When I was pregnant, I was very ill. Spent most of my pregnancy in the hospital. I had to get three pints of blood and had kidney and bladder infections. I was on a liquid diet. Finally, when I could eat regular food, Alvino came to see me at the hospital and asked me what I wanted to eat. I said, "Gorditas." So, the next day, he brought me a dozen Gorditas, and I ate them all by myself. My mom said that Alvino always spoiled me. He even tried to protect me from my mom's beatings. She even hit Alvino! He told her that she hit me too much and then she hit him. He said, "Aye Mama!" as he ducked from her hand. At one time when I was two or three and my little sister, 15 months younger than me, my mom was paralyzed. My dad worked at the Buick Garage, and my grandmother worked at the Naval Hospital in Long Beach. So, the only available person to care for my mom and us little ones was Alvino. He was out of work due to gout. He could barely walk, but he took care of us. He would have me sit on a little chair and wait for him to finish changing my little sister's diapers and helping my mom to the restroom. Alvino was the best!

On another occasion, we were at school and mom and dad were at work. Grandma was alone working in her yard; she was burning trash and accidently fell into the fire. She had no idea that Alvino was home, but she called out for Alvino and he came hobbling over and saved her from burning up. He was her hero! In C.B., we all helped each other without a second thought.

# Biographies

**Margit Andersson** was born in Sweden and has lived in Hemet for the last 13 years. She was always interested in literature and in writing. Since she retired she attended UC Riverside and obtained a degree in Anthropology. She now volunteers at the Western Center of Natural History in Hemet. Margit enjoys reading, traveling and learning new things.

**Rose Baldwin** is a Midwesterner by birth and a Californian by choice. A retired civil servant, she lives near Palm Springs with her two cats. *Mike's Magic Burger* is her second book. *The Claire Stories* was published October 2016. She is currently working on more stories and poems about Claire and her friends. Both books are available from Amazon.com.

**Larry Burns** is a writer, artist, and teacher who draws inspiration and ideas from the heady mixture of sights, sounds, peoples, and places of his hometown, Riverside CA. He enjoys writing that employs simple themes and language, allowing the reader to participate by establishing for themselves what the writing means. Living and creating from this part of the world has its pros and cons - "As a lifelong resident of the Inland Empire, sometimes my lungs seize from the diesel fumes and my eyes tell me there are no mountains to the north. But beneath the dirt lies treasure. And that treasure is mine - mine all mine!"

**Steve Brown** was born in the East Texas Piney woods in 1938. He finished school in southern New Mexico and from there went into the Navy. Always an unstoppable reader, he started to write to pass time on shipboard. Story after story flowed, each more pornographic than the last. His shipmates loved it but the Navy didn't, so his budding career as an author came to a sudden halt. Years passed and with then came the more regular elements of life. Finally in retirement, he saw a flyer for Mae Wagner Marinello's workshop and the old urge to smear ink on paper flared up again. Here we are! Wow! What fun!

**Thatcher Carter** is a fiction and creative non-fiction writer based in Riverside, CA, where she teaches at Riverside City College. Her essays have been published in *Journal of Popular Culture, 3Elements Review, Muse,* and the Riverfeet Press anthology *Awake in the World.* She was honored to participate in the Writer-to-Writer Program with the Association of Writers & Writing Programs and is working on her first novel Salt City. She lives in Riverside in an empty nest with her husband Ross and their two dogs and would take the chance to teach her teens to drive again any day.

After 35 years as a bilingual teacher, **Jose Chavez** has retired in order to write. He belongs to the Society of Children's Book Writers & Illustrators, California Association of Bilingual Educators, Inland Scribes, and Inlandia Bilingual Workshop. He has had poetry published in the *Multilingual Educator Journal* and is excited about publication of his award-winning bilingual children's book: *Estrellitas y Nopales-Little Stars and Cactus.*

An Inland Empire resident for the past 30 years, **Sylvia Clarke** has grown to appreciate the variety of activities this part of California has to offer. Her favorites include scrambling in Joshua Tree National Park, singing in a local church choir, and counting the different kinds of wildflowers she and her husband, Wil, find on walks with their dog Katie in the La Sierra Hills near their home. Since her retirement, Sylvia has enjoyed attending writing classes and Inlandia Writing Workshops because they have spurred her to spend more time writing, an aspiration since childhood.

**Wil Clarke** retired from teaching math at La Sierra University and Riverside Community College in the Inland Empire for 27 years. He enjoys scrambling on the rocks in Joshua Tree National Park and identifying flowers on the La Sierra Hills. His blog is http://wils-thoughts.blogspot.com/. He is very thankful to Inlandia, Ms. Bumpus, and Ms. Carrillo for instruction and encouragement in writing. He is excited about recent breakthroughs in the translation of the Bible into world languages that still do not have a translation. He enjoys traveling in the U.S. and abroad.

**Deenaz P. Coachbuilder, Ph. D.** is an educator, artist, poet and environmental advocate. She is a retired school principal and professor in special education, and a consulting speech pathologist. Deenaz is a Fulbright scholar, and the recipient of several awards, including a "Volunteer Service" award from President Obama. Her poetry, commentaries and essays have appeared in international, national and regional publications. Her book of poems, *Imperfect Fragments*, has been received with critical acclaim both here and abroad. Deenaz has exhibited her paintings in oil in diverse venues, including solo shows. She resides in Riverside California, Seattle Washington, and Mumbai, India. She enjoys reading, travelling, gardening, going for long walks, family and close friends, staying involved in the Indian American community, the Zoroastrian Association of California and Inlandia Institute. She particularly cherishes being a wife, mother, and a recent grandmother.

**Carlos Cortés** is a professor emeritus of history at the University of California, Riverside. His most recent books are his memoir, *Rose Hill: An Intermarriage before Its Time* (Heyday, 2012), *Multicultural America: A Multimedia Encyclopedia* (Sage, 2013), and a book of poetry, *Fourth Quarter: Reflections of a Cranky Old Man* (Bad Knee Press, 2016), which received honorable mention in the 2017 International Latino Book Awards. Cortés served as Creative/Cultural Advisor for Nickelodeon's "Dora the Explorer" and "Go, Diego, Go!," for which he received the 2009 NAACP Image Award. He also performs his one-person autobiographical play, *A Conversation with Alana: One Boy's Multicultural Rite of Passage.*

At 17, **Laurel Cortés** went to Mexico City alone to attend the University of Mexico. The experience changed her life and, after majoring in Spanish and minoring in Comparative Literature at San Diego State University, she worked for 28 years at the University of California, Riverside in--guess what?--The Department of Literatures and Languages, a job perfectly suited to her interests. Now, after a lifetime of studying and working with writers of all kinds, it's fun to do a bit of writing on her own.

**Ellen Estilai** received her B.A. in Art from the University of California, Davis, and her M. A. in English Language and Literature from the University of Tehran. A former executive director of the Riverside Arts Council and the Arts Council for San Bernardino County, she has taught literature and writing at the University of Tehran, Cal State Bakersfield and in the University of San Francisco's external degree program. Her essay, "Front Yard Fruit," originally published in *Alimentum: The Literature of Food*, is included in *New California Writing 2011* (Heyday) and was selected as a

Notable Essay in *The Best American Essays 2011*. A Pushcart Prize nominee, her poetry and essays have also appeared in the journals *Phantom Seed*, *Broad!*, *Snapdragon: A Journal of Art and Healing*, *Ink & Letters*, and *Heron Tree*, and the anthologies *Slouching Towards Mount Rubidoux Manor*, *(In)Visible Memoirs, Vol. 2.*, *Writing from Inlandia*, and *HOME: Tall Grass Writers Guild Anthology*. Ellen is a founding board member and past-president of the Inlandia Institute.

**Nan Friedley** is a retired special education teacher and graduate of Ball State University, Muncie, IN. Her writings have been published in a poetry chapbook *Short Bus Ride* by Bad Knee Press, *Indiana Voice Journal*, *Inlandia Anthologies*, and *Three* a nonfiction anthology collection by PushPenPress. Nan participates in the Riverside Inlandia Workshop.

**Alexis Gonzalez** was born and raised in San Bernardino. She is an up and coming author and poet, whose intentions with each individual work are to inspire those reading. She understands that words can be powerful tools in the healing and upliftment of others and is always looking for new ways to express the beauty that surrounds her.

**Maria Jaquez** was born in El Paso, Texas but has lived in California for 45 years and in Riverside for 32 years. She taught politics, Women's Studies and Ethnic studies at various colleges. Then, she got involved in the health recovery movement in Riverside for almost 20 years. She spent 10 years training people with mental health challenges to become peer support specialists. Her passion is cats because they're independent; they value their freedom; and are very graceful. She loves learning languages, reading, art, knitting and crochet.

**Judy Conibear Kohnen** is from neither here, nor there, but those places in between. Raised overseas in Canada, Iran and France, she is a cross-cultural writer whose works are unified by themes of identity, loss and belonging. Kohnen obtained a B.A in Psychology from McGill University, Montreal. She moved to California in 1989 and been a sales manger for several IT software start-ups. She currently works as an Administrator for her husband's engineering company. Since 2014, she has been President of the California Writers Club, Inland Empire Branch, and in 2016 she became co-chair for a grass-root volunteer group called Refugee Resettlement Team #2 working with incoming Syrian, Iraqi and Afghan refugees settling in the Pomona Valley area. She has raised a menagerie of dogs, cats, a son, a daughter, a bird and one husband. On occasion, she'll take a break from her busy life to haunt her cemetery of unfinished manuscripts and poems, located in Claremont, California, under her bed.

**Morris Frank Mendoza** was born at Riverside Community Hospital in 1948. I grew up in the neighborhood of Casa Blanca and attended Riverside schools. I have lived here my entire life. I served two years in the Army and four years in California National Guard. I've been married to Rosie for 38 years and have three children. I retired as a clerk after 40 years in the U.S. Postal Service. I've been actively involved in my community since 1970. Currently, I'm the Secretary of the VFW as an adjutant. I volunteer at Catholic Charities in the community garden, and food distribution.

**Marvin Meyer** was born on a farm in Western Oklahoma in 1936. He spent most of his early years farming there; he also became a bricklayer, a surveyor and an engineer of many types, including civil, hydraulic, flight and safety. Marvin worked as a California Registered Safety Engineer through most of his civilian work life. He also spent 34 years as an Air Force Reserve aircraft mechanic and flight engineer with over 6,000 hours in the air. Marvin currently resides in the Inland Empire with his wife, Barbara. They have been married for 58 years and raised three children.

**Rose Y. Monge** was born in Agua Prieta, Sonora, Mexico but has lived in the Riverside area since she was five. She is one of ten children-five of them are educators. She was a teacher and guidance counselor for 41 years before retiring from Poly H.S. in 2008. She is a long-life learner and values opportunities to learn and to teach others. Her parents believed in the "American Dream" that anyone can succeed if they have unwavering faith, dedication and perseverance. Everything she is is due to her parents who sacrificed their lives to bring their family to the United States.

**Kimmery Moss** graduated from USC with a bachelor's degree in creative writing/English and a minor in political science. After dedicating three years to educating at-risk middle school youth, she is now pursuing her love of writing full-time. She lives in Southern California with two rambunctious puppies and a wonderful husband.

**Cindi Neisinger** believes curiosity will lead you to your passion. Her love for the National Historic Landmark, The Mission Inn Hotel and Spa, in downtown Riverside, California, inspired her children's book, "Mouse Wedding at the Inn:Where's Daddy?", written under the pen name of CindiLoOo. She did not start off with the intention of writing. She took online writing courses, participated in a writers critique group and attended workshops through the Inlandia Institute. These courses and networking, motivated her to continue learning and improving techniques for writing. Currently, she is writing a woman's genre novel. Also, serving on the Inlandia Institutes Advisory Council.

**Gary Neuharth** lives in Redlands, California where he is a member of the Joslyn Writers Group. He has studied art, sculpture, and writing at San Bernardino College, La Sierra College, and Loma Linda University. Gary was in the Air Force during the late 1950's. While in the Air Force, he worked as a technical illustrator in Loan, France. He also taught art in service clubs and exhibited his paintings in Paris. Venice Beach, California, the Bohemian life, and the Beat Generation have inspired Gary's art and writing. Gary has published more than a hundred poems, many of which have been included in his art exhibits.

**Karl Pettway** was born in New York but moved to Detroit when he was in first grade; after that, he was shuttled between Detroit and California for most of his growing-up years. The contrast between the two environments was dramatic. His father, who lived in California, could only have his son for short periods of time and life was sweet; Karl's Detroit experiences included serial homelessness and times of near-starvation. But Karl was a dreamer and his daydreams and imagination transported him to faraway places. Although he would still love to travel to faraway places of reality, he currently lives in Redlands where he studies Mandarin and participates in the Redlands' Inlandia workshop.

**Cindy Rinne** creates art and writes in San Bernardino, CA. She brings myth to life in contemporary context. Cindy is the author of *Listen to the Codex* (Yak Press), *Breathe In Daisy, Breathe Out Stones* (FutureCycle Press), *Quiet Lantern* (Turning Point), *spider with wings* (Jamii Publishing), and she coauthored *Speaking Through Sediment* with Michael Cooper (ELJ Publications). Cindy is a founding member of

PoetrIE, an Inland Empire based literary community and a finalist for the 2016 Hillary Gravendyk Prize poetry book competition. Her poems appeared or are forthcoming in: *Birds Piled Loosely, CircleShow, Home Planet News, Outlook Springs, The Wild Word (Berlin), Storyscape Journal, Cholla Needles*, and others. www.fiberverse.com

**David Rios** hails from Maryland. While that state was home base for many years, there were excursions to Panamá—two of which entailed traveling through Central America, two school years in Argentina, one school year in France and about six years working in Mexico. With the exception of two years, he has worked in libraries since eighth grade. Currently a librarian at the University of California Riverside, he very much enjoys genealogy and soaking up local history. He serves on the Inlandia Institute Board of Directors and lives in Redlands with his wife and daughter.

**Kristine Shell** lives in Redlands, California, where she participates in the Joslyn Writers Group. Kristine is a retired school administrator and teacher. She holds a Bachelor's degree in English and Secondary Education. She also holds Master degrees in Elementary Reading and School Administration. Kristine joined the Inlandia Institute in October, 2016.

**Gabrielle Symmes** is not a writer. She's a mother, daughter, wife, grandmother, sister, and friend, who happens to share this human experience on paper every now and then. Passionate about love, life, beauty and experience. Terribly unorganized, and constantly running late because she is trying to squeeze every minute out of every day, to its fullest. She is ever hopeful, ever dreaming, ever seeking truth and knowledge and laughter and every day pleasures. She hopes to learn to play the guitar and piano, by the time she is 50, and will overcome her fear of flying, so she can see Europe with her family.

**Gudelia Vaden (Delia)** is a retired preschool teacher with a BA degree in Liberal Studies with a Bilingual-Bicultural Emphasis. She has developed several hobbies: gardening, line dancing, watercolor painting and creative writing. During the last several years, she has participated in the Inlandia Creative Writing Workshops. Delia resides in Riverside, CA with her husband Tom and granddaughter Natasha. She has a son in Riverside and her daughter lives in San Francisco. Delia and Tom enjoy walking their Chihuahua (Pepper) in their Hillcrest neighborhood.

**Tom Vaden** is a retired statistician with a MS degree in Mathematics from the University of Missouri at Columbia. He is actively involved in gardening, line dancing, and creative writing. During the last several years, he has participated in the Inlandia Creative Writing Workshops where he has learned much from the lively discussions and suggestions of the other participants. He resides in Riverside, CA with his wife Delia and a black and white very spoiled Chihuahua named Pepper. Tom has a daughter Natalie living in San Francisco, and a son Patrick living in Riverside – both are excellent writers. His granddaughter, Natasha, a graduate of the University of Oregon, lives with Delia and Tom.

**Scharlett Stowers Vai** was born and raised in Casa Blanca, a Mexican community in Riverside, California. She was raised, both as Black and Chicana by an entire community. She attended Casa Blanca Elementary School, Matthew Gage Jr. High School, and Ramona High School. She attended UC Riverside and Riverside City College, majoring in Early Childhood Studies. She taught at Casa Blanca State Preschool for 11 years. She spends much of her time at Ysmael Villegas Community Center. Scharlett is very proud to have grown up in Casa Blanca for 65 years now.

**Alan VanTassel** grew up in Northern Illinois, graduated from DeKalb Senior High School, and Northern Illinois University. Alan spent his four-year enlistment at Naval Air Station, Point Mugu, CA. On separation from the military Alan returned to Illinois and began teaching in a town called Harvard. In 1991 Alan found a teaching position in the Colton Joint Unified School District at Colton Middle School. He stayed there until he transferred to Bloomington High School in 1996, then in 2003 he went to Moreno Valley High School, then the following two years at Victor Valley High School, then finally Banning High School, where he taught for 11 years. Alan retired in June, 2017. Alan lives with his wife, Sarah, in Redlands, CA.

**Dale Vassantachart** grew up in Hawaii and now resides in Colton, California. Through her writings, she would like to make children smile, think, and learn. Dale receives encouragement from writers in Inlandia Creative Writing Workshop and a small poetry group near her home. Dale completed a doctorate degree in education and is a former clinician and educator in occupational therapy. Her husband and family can be seen hiking the trails in the Inland Empire and sharing the wonders of nature with others.

**Frances J. Vasquez** is a native of the Inlandia region. She pursued higher education at Riverside City College and the University of California, Riverside where she earned BS and MBA Degrees. She wrote her Master's Thesis on the status of Chicano leadership. She has a diverse background in public service and served as International Director/CEO of Other Cultures, Inc., a student exchange program focused on México, Central America, Canada, and the U.S. An aficionada of arts and letters, she appreciates attending and organizing cultural events. She serves as past president of the Inlandia Institute.

**Romaine Washington** is the author of *Sirens in Her Belly*, Jamii Publishing 2015. The collection of poems was placed on BET's must-read list in 2016. She is a fellow of The Watering Hole, South Carolina and the Inland Area Writing Project, University California Riverside.

# About the Inlandia Institute

The Inlandia Institute is a regional non-profit literary center. We seek to bring focus to the richness of the literary enterprise that has existed in this region for ages. The mission of the Inlandia Institute is to recognize, support and expand literary activity in all of its forms through community programs in the Inland Southern California, thereby deepening people's awareness, understanding, and appreciation of this unique, complex and creatively vibrant region.

The Institute publishes high quality regional writing in print and electronic form including books published in partnership with Heyday under the Inlandia Institute imprint as well as independent Inlandia Institute publications. The Inlandia Institute is also home to the Hillary Gravendyk prize, a national and regional poetry book competition.

Inlandia presents free public literary programming featuring authors who live in, work in, and/or write about Inland Southern California.

We also provide Creative Literacy Programs for children and youth and hold creative writing workshops for teens and adults.

In addition, every two years the Inlandia Institute appoints a distinguished jury panel from outside of the region to name an Inlandia Literary Laureate who serves as an ambassador for the Inlandia Institute, promoting literature, creative literacy, and community throughout the entire Inlandia region. To date, Laureates include Susan Straight (2010-12), Gayle Brandeis (2012-14), Juan Delgado (2014-16), and Nikia Chaney (2016-2018).

To learn more about the Inlandia Institute please visit our website at www.InlandiaInstitute.org.

# Other Inlandia Publications

**Inlandia Books - Literary**
*Go to the Living*
Micha Chatterton

*Traces of a Fifth Column*
Marco Maisto
Winner of the 2016 National Hillary Gravendyk Prize

*God's Will for Monsters*
Rachelle Cruz
Winner of the 2016 Regional Hillary Gravendyk Prize

*Map of an Onion*
Kenji C. Liu
Winner of the 2015 National Hillary Gravendyk Prize

*All Things Lose Thousands of Times*
Angela Peñaredondo
Winner of the 2015 Regional Hillary Gravendyk Prize

**Inlandia Books - Community**
*While We're Here We Should Sing*
The Why Nots

*No Easy Way: Integrating Riverside Schools - A Victory for Community*
Arthur L. Littleworth
Edited by Dawn Hassett
Foreword by Dr. V.P. Franklin
Introduction by Susan Straight

*Tia's Tamale Trouble*
Julianna Cruz, author
Tracie Lents, illustrator

*Orangelandia: The Literature of Inland Citrus*
Edited by Gayle Brandeis

*Dos Chiles/Two Chilies*
Julianna Cruz

*Yearly, 2011-2016 Writing from Inlandia:*
*Work of the Inlandia Creative Writing Writing Workshops*
Edited by the Inlandia Institute Publications Committee

**Heyday Inlandia Imprint Books**
*Empire*
Lewis deSoto

*Vital Signs*
Juan Delgado and Thomas McGovern

*Rose Hill: An Intermarriage before Its Time*
Carlos Cortès

*No Place for a Puritan: The Literature of California's Deserts*
Edited by Ruth Nolan

*Backyard Birds of the Inland Empire*
Sheila N. Kee

*Dream Street*
Douglas F. McCulloh

*Inlandia: A Literary Journey Through California's Inland Empire*
Edited by Gayle Wattawa with an introduction by Susan Straight

**Inlandia Electronic Publications**
*Inlandia: A Literary Journey, an on-line journal*
Edited by Lawrence Eby

www.ingramcontent.com/pod-product-compliance
Lightning Source LLC
Chambersburg PA
CBHW020847090426
42736CB00008B/275